THE FRENCH REVOLUTION

AND

ENGLISH LITERATURE

THE

FRENCH REVOLUTION

AND

ENGLISH LITERATURE

LECTURES DELIVERED IN CONNECTION WITH THE
SESQUICENTENNIAL CELEBRATION OF
PRINCETON UNIVERSITY

BY

EDWARD DOWDEN *1843 - 1913*

LL.D., LITT. D. (DUBLIN), HON. LL.D. (EDINBURGH), HON. D.C.L. (OXFORD).
HON. LL.D. (PRINCETON), PROFESSOR OF ENGLISH LITERATURE
IN THE UNIVERSITY OF DUBLIN

KENNIKAT PRESS, INC./PORT WASHINGTON, N. Y.

820.9

PREFACE

THE substance of this volume was embodied in lectures given in Trinity College, Cambridge, when I had the honor to hold the Clark Lectureship in English Literature. On receiving the honor of an invitation from the authorities of Princeton University to deliver a series of lectures in connection with the Sesqui-centennial Celebration, I revised my material and made some additions. It is the wish of those who organized and carried out that brilliant Celebration that these lectures should be published; and I am further encouraged to publication by the great kindness of many of my American fellow-students, and by the generous welcome which I received from an American audience. I think of my days spent in the autumn of last year at that old and distinguished seat of learning, which has contributed so much to the best life of the United States, with a feeling of happy gratitude.

In these lectures I go over some ground which I have previously traversed; the point of view, perhaps, gives unity to the results of various studies. I do not attempt to prove a thesis. I have tried to enter in a disinterested way into the spirit of each writer who comes within the scope of my subject, and to let the meanings of the French Revolution, as they entered into English literature, expound themselves. To present some important figures on a background of history — history of ideas rather than of events — has been my aim.

I have acknowledged a debt to M. Angellier in what I say of Burns, and to M. Legouis in some things which I say of Wordsworth. A passage of the last lecture is reclaimed from an article of my own contributed to a magazine.

E. D.

Trinity College, Dublin,
January 7, 1897.

CONTENTS

I

PRECURSORS OF REVOLUTION

THE FRENCH REVOLUTION AND ENGLISH LITERATURE

———•———

I

PRECURSORS OF REVOLUTION

BEFORE the stream of Revolutionary thought and feeling gathered to flow in a channel, its diffused substance existed in the form of what may be described as a mist. From a fortunate distance certain wreathings of that mist may be observed. Taine, in the opening volume of his book on the "Origins of Contemporary France," resolves into two chief elements the Revolutionary spirit: first, the progress of natural and experimental science, with the application of the methods of science to the study of human society and human history; secondly, the classical tendency, which reduces the particular and individual to general ideas, or substitutes an abstraction for a group of things concrete with all their manifold details. The second

of these influences was active in England, — we
feel its presence in such a book as Godwin's "Political Justice," — but it had not in our country, as it
had in France, the weight of a predominant tradition, and the character of the English mind held it
in check.   The acquisitions and the methods of
science deeply affected the temper and habits of
thought in both countries.   In astronomy, in
optics, in chemistry, in geology and mineralogy,
in botany, in zoölogy, in physiology, great names
make the eighteenth century illustrious; great discoveries were co-ordinated under ruling ideas. But
is not man a portion of nature ? And if so,
why should not the ideas and methods of science
be applied to the study of man as an individual,
to the study of society and of its development ?
It was not authority, it was not conceptions inherited from the past, which had given this
powerful impetus to scientific discovery ; these
had been reversed or set aside. Reason had
taken the place of authority. Why should not
reason also become supreme in the study of
humanity, and in all arrangements for the social
and political life of man ? Why should there
not be a mathematics dealing with the units,
and groups of units, which make up society ?
Why should not society be established, though

now for the first time, on the basis of reason ? Might this not be, if only authority and prescription, customs and conventions, inherited beliefs and the prejudices of ignorance, were once for all displaced or overthrown ? The new faith in reason became an enthusiasm with something of the force of a new religion.

An idea of unlimited human progress had been generated by the vast scientific movement of the century. Man is not a perfect creature, but surely he is perfectible; and the motive-power in his endless advance can be no other than the human reason. But in order that reason may have full scope and play, absolute freedom is essential, a complete emancipation from prejudice must be attained. The chain of inference appeared to be unbroken and strong ; " Is it possible for us," asked Godwin, " to contemplate what man has already done, without being impressed with a strong presentiment of the improvements he has yet to accomplish ? There is no science that is not capable of additions ; there is no art that may not be carried to a still higher perfection. If this be true of all other sciences, why not of morals ? If this be true of all other arts, why not of social institution ? The very conception of this as possible is in the highest degree encouraging. If we can still further demonstrate it to be a part of the natural and regular progress of mind, our confidence and our hopes will then be complete. This is the temper with which we ought to engage in the study of political truth." The same doctrine has been taught to our own generation, and has been pushed even farther in the direction of homage to the reason. In Draper's ambitious work the author stated, in language which is strange as coming from a professedly scientific writer, that Nature, the abstraction Nature, has an aim, and that this aim is not a moral but an intellectual development. Buckle, in his "History of Civilization," maintained that the intellectual element is the dynamic force in society, having an activity and a capacity for adaptation which make it the chief mover in an indefinite progress of humanity. It is perhaps worth noting, as a symptom of one tendency of thought in our own day, that a recent contribution to the study of Social Evolution, that by Mr. Benjamin Kidd, argues on grounds, which claim to be scientific, in favor of a theory precisely the opposite to that of Buckle. The conclusion which Darwinian science must eventually establish is, in Mr. Kidd's view, that the evolution slowly proceeding in human society has primarily a religious rather than an intellectual character.

However this may be, the eighteenth century, the *sæculum rationalisticum*, believed, as a cardinal article of faith, in the supremacy of reason as an agent in the progress of society. This belief was nourished and sustained by the great scientific discoveries of the age ; and it tended to produce that assurance or that dream of the possibility of boundless advance for the race, which formed part of the Revolutionary creed, and which was summed up in the expression *human perfectibility*. The new evangel had its apostles and prophets and martyrs. There is something sublime and something pathetic in their unalterable optimism. The most glowing words, perhaps, celebrating the promised golden age, seen in vision from the undelectable mountains of Revolution, were written by the proscribed Condorcet in the closing pages of his unfinished " Progrès de l'Esprit humain." The contemplation of the happier future of humanity he describes as a refuge for the philosopher, into which the recollection of his persecutors can never follow him, — " in which living in thought with man reinstated in the rights and the dig-

nity of his nature, he forgets man tormented and
corrupted by greed, by base fear, by envy." "It
is here," cries Condorcet, "that he truly abides
with his fellows, in an elysium which his reason
has known how to create for itself, and which
his love for humanity adorns with all purest
delights." Condorcet's sympathetic critic, Mr.
Morley, admits that the "Progrès de l'Esprit
humain" fails to consider the history of moral
improvement, and is seriously marred by the
philosopher's angry and vehement hostility to
the religions of the world.

But the eighteenth century was not merely
a *sæculum rationalisticum*. There had been in
England, as well as in France and Germany, a
great enfranchisement of the passions. There
had been a great outbreak of religious emotions in
the movement which was represented by White-
field and Wesley. In literature the sentimental
movement, of which the spirit is present in such
representative works as Rousseau's "La nouvelle
Héloïse," Goethe's "Werther," and Sterne's "Tris-
tram Shandy," ran its course, and probably would
have perished through its own excesses, had it
not turned somewhat away from literature and
coalesced with the new philanthropy of the
time. The worship of passion, the abandonment

to sentiment, had been dissolvents of moral and social order; the first of duties was no longer to act aright, but to be touched by a delicate distress. Yet under the affectations of the sentimentalists lay a real refining of human sympathy. In its more robust form the tender emotion of the time passed into the new philanthropy; and among the sources which went to form the Revolutionary stream this is not the least important. The cause of Revolution seemed to many thinkers, and especially to the younger and more ardent spirits, to be the cause of humanity. The laws were harsh, and were administered with little pity; the criminal, generous or amiable, became a favorite with imaginative writers. Human nature — so it had been eloquently preached — is essentially good; the unreasonable and unfeeling arrangements of society are the chief causes of crime. All that philanthropy had been striving for in this direction and in that was to be attained in its unity and completeness by the Revolution. When the Bastille fell, what was this but the fulfilment of the unaccomplished work of John Howard? Fox only gave expression to the sentiment of many of his contemporaries when he exclaimed, " How much the greatest event it is that ever happened in the

world! and how much the best!" Not that as
a fact the fall of the Bastille quite enfranchised
the whole of humanity; it had held in confinement seven prisoners, four of whom were accused
of forgery; one was an idiot; one was detained
at the request of his family; while, on the other
hand, the bodies of upwards of fourscore dead
compatriots lay in the governor's court, and
certain heads were borne in triumph on the
pikes of fraternity. But the Bastille served well
enough as a symbol for the imagination; its ruins
typified the ashes of the old régime; and from
those ashes the phœnix of human happiness and
freedom seemed to rise. Philanthropy was entering on its revolutionary apotheosis, when the
evangel of humanity was most clearly to be read
if it were written in blood.

But in the days before this apotheosis imagination had also played its part, and it was
set upon defining certain actual evils, and ascer-
taining the way to practical reforms. The Penal
Code of England was still one of savage severity,
and little had been done to amend its provisions.
It was something when in 1783 the cruel pro-
cession to Tyburn was abolished. And at least
one great statesman, — but he proved himself to
be no admirer of the French Revolution, — Ed-

mund Burke, pleaded for a revisal of that code, which he described as abominable. The great work of Howard's life on behalf of prison reform began with his appointment, in 1773, as High Sheriff of Bedfordshire. His personal inspection of prisons was carried out under circumstances which involved on his own part heroic fortitude, in which he was supported not only by his passion of humanity, but by a deep sense of religious duty. Indeed, the example of Howard and that of Wilberforce are instances of the debt which the philanthropic movement of the eighteenth and nineteenth centuries owed to the Evangelical revival. Howard did his work patiently and well, thoroughly informing the public as to the condition of the prisoner and his wretched abode, — the scanty food, the lack of warmth, the overcrowding, the poisonous atmosphere, the consequent diseases, the untended condition of the sick, the ponderous chains and iron collars, the fees extorted by unpaid jailers, the languishing for years of those incarcerated for petty debts.

Among the philanthropic efforts of the time, that on behalf of the abolition of the slave-trade was the most considerable. Into it entered something of the Revolutionary feeling for liberty, and yet more of the sentiment of fraternity. As early as 1668 William Penn had denounced the cruelty of the trade, and his successors in the Society of Friends had never been quite insensible to its evils. The exertions of the Quakers, in days preceding the great upheaval in France, were ably seconded by Granville Sharp, Clarkson, and Wilberforce, members of the Church of England. Evidence was collected by Clarkson; the system of kidnapping, the native wars that fed the trade, the horrors of the Middle Passage, were exposed; and on this subject at least there was no serious difference of opinion between Pitt and Fox and Burke. In 1780 Burke prepared a code for the mitigation and ultimate abolishment of the traffic in human lives, but he lost hope in the possibility of bringing it to a successful issue. In 1788 he "spoke strongly to the effect that the trade was one which ought to be totally abolished, but if this was not now possible, it ought to be regulated at once. All delay in such a matter was criminal." [1] It is melancholy to recall the fact that the direct cause why this reform was not attained before the close of the eighteenth century was that violent outbreak on behalf of freedom, in which its admirers saw the immediate emancipation of the world. In

[1] Lecky, England in the Eighteenth Century, vol. vi. p. 291.

the panic created by the French Revolution the interests of the oppressed Africans receded. Danton declared that slavery had been abolished in the French colonies in order that the negroes in the colonies of England and Spain might be excited to revolt. The century, in the words of Mr. Lecky, "terminated with the temporary defeat of a cause which twelve years before seemed on the eve of triumph." Nevertheless, the younger spirits of the Revolutionary movement in our literature, and in particular Southey, remained ardent champions of negro emancipation.

The idea of progress and human perfectibility, the humanitarian passion, — we have seen how these entered into the Revolutionary spirit before the Revolution. A third element which entered into that spirit produced remarkable effects in literature as well as in life. Mr. Morley has said that the keynote of the Revolutionary time is expressed by the word "simplification." The Revolution was, or aimed at being, as we are often told, "a return to nature." Return to nature, — it is an elastic word which is capable of many meanings. When Pope and Addison pleaded for a return to nature, they meant a return to good sense, the common intelligence, and the observation of actual life in place of the fantastic ingenuities of false wit and the eccentricities of private conceit. Now the meaning was different. The "return to nature" signified a simplification in social life in contrast with the artificialities and conventions which had accumulated in a highly complex age, and especially in cities and in courts; a sigh, genuine or affected, for the simplicities of rural existence, or it might be for "a lodge in some vast wilderness;" a fresh delight in beauty of the mountain and the woods; a discovery of the dignity of human passions in the shepherd and the tiller of the soil; a recognition in politics of the rights of man as man, regardless of the claims of aristocratic caste or class; an assertion of unbounded freedom for the individual, or a freedom limited only by such duties as were imposed by universal fraternity. In these and in other respects, the Revolution professed to simplify life. As a young man, Fox had worn elegant costumes, red-heeled shoes, and blue hair-powder; during the American war he and his friends distinguished themselves by a studious indifference to the refinements of dress. "From the House of Commons," says Wraxall, "and the clubs of St. James's Street it spread through the private assemblies of London. But though gradually undermined and insensibly perishing of an atrophy, dress never totally fell till the era of Jacobinism and of Equality in 1793 and 1794." "This period," writes Mr. Lecky, "marks a complete revolution in English dress. It was then that the picturesque cocked hat went out of fashion. . . . Then, too, the silver buckle was exchanged for the ordinary shoe-tie. Muslin cravats, pantaloons, and Hessian boots came into fashion, and the mode of dressing the hair was wholly changed. Like the Roundheads of the seventeenth century, the democrats of the eighteenth century adopted the fashion of cutting the hair short, and they also discarded as inconsistent with republican simplicity that hair-powder which, since the abolition of wigs, had been invariably worn by the upper classes. It is interesting to notice that among the young students of Oxford who were foremost in taking this step, were Southey and Savage Landor."[1] Then, too, the powder and paint of poetic diction were discarded by the younger poets; it was declared that the actual language of common discourse sufficed for the highest needs of literature, and that the best part of our vocabulary is that which can be gathered from the lips of peasants who

[1] England in the Eighteenth Century, vol. vi. pp. 147, 148.

are accustomed to express their feelings with
simplicity, and who live in communion with
the majestic and ennobling presence of external
nature.

An indication of the turn which feeling was
taking in the direction of simplification as regards
social life is found long before the Revolution,
as early as 1757, in a book which in its own day
made a considerable stir, — Brown's "Estimate
of the Manners and Principles of the Times." It
speedily passed through several editions. "The
inestimable Estimate of Brown," says one of the
speakers in Cowper's "Table-Talk," "rose like a
paper kite and charmed the town;" and indeed
the town from time to time enjoys hearing its
own vices or foibles criticised or satirized. The
book is a protest against the luxury and effeminacy of the age. Two merits Brown allows to
Englishmen, — they value liberty and they possess humanity; for the rest they deserve little
but censure. Some sentences from Mr. Leslie
Stephen's summary of the indictment brought
against his countrymen by Brown will sufficiently
indicate the drift of the writer: "At our schools
the pupils learn words, not things; on the grand
tour young men contract foreign vices without
widening their minds; money is lavished on

foreign cookery instead of being spent on plain English fare; conversation is trivial or vicious; silly plays, novels, and pamphlets have replaced works of solid literature; the fine arts are depraved; opera and pantomime are preferred to Shakespeare's plays; men's principles are as bad as their manners; religion is universally ridiculed, yet the fashionable irreligion is shallow; vices are laughed at on the stage, and are repeated at home without a blush; the professions are corrupt, except law which ministers to the selfish, and physic which assists the effeminate; politicians are mere jobbers; officers are gamblers and bullies; the clergy are contemned and are contemptible; low spirits and nervous disorders have notoriously increased, until the people of England are no longer capable of self-defence." [1] And so the indictment, with many counts, proceeds. Brown was no revolutionist; but he gave an early expression to the feeling in favor of simplification which was part of the Revolutionary mode of feeling. The sentiment was far more powerfully expressed, if also with certain extravagances of theory from which Brown is free, by Rousseau; and Rousseau, who was a

[1] L. Stephen, English Thought in the Eighteenth Century, vol. ii. pp. 195, 196 (abbreviated).

chief inspirer of the doctrine and the passions of Revolution, gained a not inconsiderable following in England.

Johnson, who stood on the old ways, who suspected novelties of thought and scorned whatever seemed to be sentimental nonsense, maintained that the dread of luxury was visionary. " Luxury," he declared, " so far as it reaches the poor, will do good to the race of people; it will strengthen and multiply them.   Sir, no nation was ever hurt by luxury, for it can reach but to a very few."   And he went on to challenge Goldsmith to take a walk from Charing Cross to Whitechapel, examining the shops with a view to investigating which of them sold anything, except it were gin, that could harm any human being.   " Well, sir," answered Goldsmith, " I 'll accept your challenge.   The very next shop to Northumberland House is a pickle-shop."   Johnson, as usual, when brought to bay, rose to the height of the great argument: " Well, sir, do we not know that a maid can in one afternoon make pickles sufficient to serve a whole family for a year; nay, that five pickle-shops can serve all the kingdom ?   Besides, sir, there is no harm done to anybody by the making of pickles, or the eating of pickles."   In 1767 John Wesley wrote in his

Journal: "I had a conversation with an ingenious man who proved to a demonstration that it was the duty of every man that could to be 'clothed in purple and fine linen' and to 'fare sumptuously every day;' and that he would do abundantly more good hereby than he could do by 'feeding the hungry and clothing the naked.' Oh the depth of human understanding! What may not a man believe if he will?" The ingenious acquaintance of Wesley, who held that private extravagances are public benefits, was adopting the same line of argument as that which Johnson, thirty-three years previously, had introduced in one of his "Debates," and some ten years afterwards repeated in conversation when he maintained that it did more good to eat a dish of green peas at half a guinea than to give the same sum to the poor, who might not be, like the market-gardener, industrious.[1] Wesley's protest against luxury is repeated on the eve of the Revolution, by Hannah More, in her "Thoughts on the Importance of the Manners of the Great to General Society" (1788). Hannah More was a reformer, but she did not desire the overthrow of thrones and of churches; her pamphlet, "Village Politics," in which the conservative

[1] Boswell's Johnson, ed. G. B. Hill. vol. iii. p. 56 and note.

working-man, Jack Anvil, a blacksmith, convicts the Jacobin working-man, Tom Hod, a mason, of the error of his ways, had a wide circulation in the year 1793. But the tendency towards simplification passed beyond the Revolutionary group. With Hannah More it was allied to her religious convictions; while admitting as Brown had done the humanity of the time, she mourns over the neglect of religious duties by persons commonly esteemed as "a good kind of people," and over "this voluptuous age, when a frivolous and relaxing dissipation has infected our very studies," and infidelity itself will not be at the trouble of deep research.

In the voluptuous age, however, some Stoics were to be found. The student of eighteenth-century literature cannot afford to overlook a book which has had probably a larger number of readers than any other work of the period; he may find something of the spirit of the time embodied in that edifying manual for youth, "Sandford and Merton." Thomas Day, the author of that exciting narrative, and Day's intimate friend, the father of Maria Edgeworth, were deeply influenced by the views on education put forth in Rousseau's "Émile." As a genuine child of nature, Émile is to be reared, yet with all the tenderness of an innocent and rural home. He is to be beguiled by amiable stratagems into acquiring knowledge. He is never to be the victim of punishment inflicted as such. The room which he occupies is to be as simple as that of a peasant. He is to think with a just abhorrence of the luxury of extravagant banquets. He may be indulged in a preference for bright colors in dress, but the material chosen must be plain and of enduring fabric. His wants must be reduced to a minimum. He must learn a trade, — that of a carpenter, if it be convenient. The book, as Mr. Morley justly observes, was an expression of the democratic tendency in education. Richard Lovell Edgeworth's eldest son was born in 1764. The father determined to make a fair trial of Rousseau's system, and a compliant mother agreed that the child should, as far as possible, be formed, both in body and mind, by the benignant powers of nature. He wore no stockings; his arms were bare; he became fearless of danger, and capable of enduring many privations. "He had," writes the father, "all the virtues of a child bred in the hut of a savage, and all the knowledge of *things* which could well be acquired at an early age by a boy bred in civilized society. I say knowledge of *things*, for of books he had less knowledge at seven or eight than most children have at four or five." Yet with these rare advantages, the experiment, somehow, did not prove a complete success. He showed himself to be, in the strictest sense of the word, a liberty-boy, a young Revolutionist; "he was not," says his father, "disposed to obey; . . . he had little deference for others, and he showed an invincible dislike to control." The Harry Sandford of Edgeworth's friend, Day, was a boy of happier disposition, "the most obliging, honest creature in the world," full of the tenderest benevolence, and so courageous that on one memorable occasion he plucked "with as much dexterity as resolution" the snake from round Master Tommy Merton's leg. Young Sandford had a true republican simplicity of manners; he was not like many other children who place their whole happiness in eating; give him but a morsel of dry bread for his dinner and he would be satisfied, though you placed sweetmeats and fruit and every other dainty in his way. He considered his father's horn flagons to be superior to Mrs. Merton's silver cup. When Mr. Merton asked Harry, "Should you like to be rich, my dear?" the admirable boy answered, "No, indeed, sir, because the only rich man I ever saw is Squire Chase, who lives hard by; and he rides among people's corn, and breaks down their hedges, and shoots their poultry, and kills their dogs, and lames their cattle, and abuses the poor; and they say he does all this because he's rich." "But should you not like to have a fine coat," — so proceeds the test of virtue,— "and a coach to carry you about, and servants to wait on you?" "As to that, madam," the youthful Stoic replies, "one coat is as good as another, if it will but keep me warm; and I don't want to ride, because I can walk wherever I choose; and as to servants, I should have nothing for them to do, if I had hundreds of them."

In the main, the type of mind which the English eighteenth century tended to produce was of the common-sense, prosaic kind, often ardently benevolent, but not carried away by extremes of passion or extravagances of imagination. When the new ideas of the second half of the century, the Revolutionary ideas, struck upon such a mind, the effects were strange. The prose and the poetry did not always happily blend together. If the man were somewhat deficient in a sense of the ridiculous, his case was worse; if he were prone to experiment and to the direct application of his ideas to life, these new ideas might lead him through the strangest of dances. It was an experimental age; the great Erasmus Darwin's definition of a fool was a man who does not venture to make an experiment. There is no one more dangerous or more diverting than the man of prosaic common-sense, who is devoid of imagination and of humor in a saving degree, and who, having an experimental turn, becomes possessed by new ideas. He will play such tricks before high Heaven as might wreathe with smiles the faces of the most serious angels. And this, in truth, was what happened with the excellent Thomas Day. He was a worthy eighteenth-century Briton, essentially prosaic, though much out of the common in the degree of his benevolence and generosity; and the burning rays from Rousseau's "Nouvelle Héloïse," "Contrat social," and "Émile" fell direct upon his British brain. He resolved to cultivate the life of simplicity and nature; hair-powder he abhorred; even comb and brush were enervating luxuries; it was sufficient to let his raven locks sway in the running brook. Although insensible to the attractions of womanhood, scornful of elegant domestic accomplishments and regardless of female beauty, except, it is confessed, the attraction of large and white arms (for there is always some weak point in a philosopher's panoply), Day arrived at the rational con-

clusion that he ought to take to himself a wife.
He accompanied Edgeworth to Ireland, where his
sentiment in favor of savage life was somewhat
disturbed by the misery of the bogland hovels;
and he would gladly have converted Edgeworth's
sister into Mrs. Thomas Day. Unluckily she
had a prejudice against unconventional manners; she did not perceive the advantages of her
suitor's simple and natural manner of eating
food, and she preferred hair that had been submitted to the comb. When, a year later, the de-
cision against her suitor was announced, Day
determined that the next time he would take
securities against failure: he would rear from
childhood two girls, chosen from among found-
ling orphans; he would instruct them in all the
wisdom of Nature and Rousseau, until she who
approached the nearer to the true standard of
perfection should be honored by becoming his
wife. One, the brunette, he called Lucretia; the
other, Sabrina Sidney, was named after the river-
goddess of the Severn and that eminent republican, Algernon Sidney. Day took his pupils to
France, as an appropriate place where they might
learn to despise dress and luxury, fine people and
fashion. But, according to the testimony of Miss
Seward, the Swan of Lichfield, they gave their

patron much trouble and quarrelled with each other. The Roman heroine, Lucretia, was found to be invincibly stupid, or, what amounted to the same, unwilling to follow Day's regimen; she was placed with a milliner, and in time married a linen-draper. Sabrina Sidney grew into a pleasing girl of engaging countenance, wearing her auburn ringlets without powder or pomatum. Yet still Day had a few things against her; when, to give her hardihood, he fired pistols at her petticoats, Sabrina screamed; when he dropped melted sealing-wax on her large and white arms, she started. Finally, she did, or she did not, wear certain long sleeves which had been the subject of his aversion or his liking; and Day, regarding this as a fatal proof of her want of strength of mind, quitted her forever. It is sad to relate that, for the sake of Miss Elizabeth Sneyd, the philosopher squandered seven or eight hours each day in learning to dance, to fence, to manage the great horse, together with every other species of artificial torture, only to be informed, when with all his accomplishments he returned from Lyons to Lichfield, that Elizabeth preferred "the blackguard" that he had been to "the fine gentleman" who now appeared in her presence. At length Day found his fate, and it was a happy

one. Miss Milnes was a person of unbounded
benevolence and of an understanding so superior
that her friends named her Minerva; the only
serious objection to his union with her was that
Miss Milnes was encumbered with a fortune.
Mrs. Day was delicate, and under her husband's
advice walking in the snow was tried as a natural
remedy; he allowed her no servants, and forbade
the enervating harpsichord; but he built for her a
dressing-room, and found that he had omitted to
leave any space for the admission of light or air.
Mr. Day, as Edgeworth says, at last fell a victim
to his own benevolence. He observed that horses
suffer much in the breaking, and decided for
himself to apply the pedagogic principles of Rousseau to equine training; the author of "Sandford
and Merton" was thrown on his head, and received a fatal concussion of the brain. His wife
died two years later, and, it is said, of a broken
heart.

Day, like his Lichfield friend Erasmus Darwin,
was a reformer in politics. He was strongly on
the side of America when the Colonies revolted
from the mother country. He advocated an en-
largement of the basis of Parliamentary representation. His addresses were published by the
Constitutional Society; but he did not seek a seat

in the House of Commons, preferring, as **Mr.** Leslie Stephen puts it, "to take Cincinnatus as his model." Before the outbreak of the French Revolution there had been in English politics a considerable popular agitation, which connected itself with American Independence and with the affair of Wilkes. Democratic teaching had been undertaken with great vigor and with no small effect by Paine, whose "Common Sense" (1776) had a large circulation, in England as well as in America. Starting from the doctrine that the more simple anything is the less likely it is to be disordered, and the easier it is to repair if disordered, Paine violently attacked the English Constitution as a complex system, compounded, with some new republican materials, from two ancient tyrannies, — the remains of monarchical tyranny in the person of the king, and the remains of aristocratical tyranny in the persons of the peers. "In England," according to Paine's "Common Sense," "the king hath little more to do than to make war and give away places; which in plain terms is to impoverish the people and set it together by the ears. A pretty business, indeed, for a man to be allowed £800,000 a year for, and worshipped into the bargain! Of more worth is one honest man to society, and in the sight of God, than all the crowned ruffians that ever lived." It would lead us away from literature were we to trace the efforts made by Cartwright and others on behalf of Parliamentary reform, annual Parliaments, the ballot, universal suffrage, or to bring under review the various democratic associations which rose and fell and rose again. Naturally dissenters, who had suffered from religious disabilities and who hated the tithe-system, constituted a large proportion of the reforming body. Alike through his scientific pursuits, his confidence in intellectual progress, his eminent position among Unitarians, and his connection with a centre of manufacturing industry, Priestley was prepared to sympathize with the forward movement in politics. Dr. Price, whose sermon before the Revolution Society gave occasion to Burke's "Reflections on the French Revolution," belonged to the same religious persuasion. Jebb, who worked with Cartwright, was in holy orders; but he resigned his preferments, and passed over to the theological position of Priestley. Thomas Christie, who was employed by the Assembly on the polyglot edition of the new constitution, was the nephew of a Presbyterian minister who withdrew from the communion of his fathers, preached to the first Unitarian congregation established in Scotland, and followed Priestley to America. William Frend, of Jesus College, whose influence on Coleridge when a student at Cambridge was considerable, and who took a zealous part in reform, both political and ecclesiastical, became in 1787 a convert to Unitarianism; six years later he was banished from the University. The same temper of mind that led to free speculation in religion showed itself in political speculation which sought to replace tradition by ideas of the reason. Unsuccessful attempts were made on the eve of the French Revolution to obtain a repeal of the Test and Corporation Acts; the forces of conservation and the forces of change were knit in a struggle for supremacy.

But when we turn to pure literature, and look for the writer who, undesignedly and unawares, was the chief representative of Revolutionary sentiment in days before the Revolution, it is remarkable that we find that representative — at least so far as concerns the humanitarian feeling and the tendency towards simplification — in one who was a devout member of the Evangelical revival in the Church of England, one of a gentle, unaggressive, yet manly temper, the poet Cowper. By his family connections Cowper was a Whig,

and at all times was ready to express the correct
Whig sentiments on the theme of British freedom. In a note appended to a passage of "The
Task" he defends himself for what might be
thought unnecessary warmth in the praise of
freedom ; "he is aware," he says, "that it is become almost fashionable to stigmatize such sentiments as no better than empty declamation ;
but it is an ill symptom, and peculiar to modern
times. When the Revolution came, Cowper was
close upon his sixtieth year, — a period of life at
which new causes are not often adopted with
ardor. His mind was much preoccupied with
the crusade against slavery. When Paine's
"Rights of Man" was offered to him, he refused
to open the book; "no man," he writes to Lady
Hesketh, "shall convince me that I am improp-
erly governed, while I feel the contrary." "The
dissenters, I think," he writes again, "Catholics
and others, have all a right to the privileges of
all other Englishmen, because to deprive them is
persecution ; and persecution on any account,
but especially on a religious one, is an abomination.
But, after all, *valeat respublica.* I love my country, I love my king, and I wish peace and prosperity to Old England." In an early poem,
"Table Talk," after suggesting that the British

love of freedom arises from the vigor induced by
a stern climate, Cowper had described the French
in the same spirit as that in which they were
represented by Goldsmith in " The Traveller ;"
they are slaves, but so light and bright of temper that they do not feel the oppression of
slavery, —

> " The Frenchman, easy, debonair, and brisk,
>   Give him his lass, his fiddle, and his frisk,
>   Is always happy, reign whoever may,
>   And laughs the sense of misery far away."

Something of the same conception of the
French people appears in a letter of December,
1792, to Lady Hesketh, in which the writer
speaks of them as vain and childish, " conduct-
ing themselves on this great occasion with a levity
and extravagance nearly akin to madness." He
thinks it were better if Austria and Prussia had
let France alone ; he declares himself in favor of
the doctrine of the sovereignty of the people as
self-evident, — " whenever the people choose to
be masters they always are so, and none can
hinder them." " God grant that we may have
no revolution here," he goes on ; " but unless we
have a reform we certainly shall. Depend upon it,
my dear, the hour is come when power founded
on patronage and corrupt majorities must govern

this land no longer." The poet of Olney was a
more masculine spirit than is commonly supposed,
and when he advocated reform he did so with the
seriousness of his mature age. Six years before
that event hailed by Fox as the greatest and the
best that the world had ever known, Cowper
looked forward with ardent desire to the hour
when the Bastille should be a ruin : —

> " Ye horrid towers, the abode of broken hearts,
>   Ye dungeons, and ye cages of despair,
>   That monarchs have supplied from age to age
>   With music such as suits their sovereign ears,
>   The sighs and groans of miserable men !
>   There 's not an English heart that would not leap
>   To hear that ye are fallen at last ; to know
>   That even our enemies so oft employed
>   In forging chains for us, themselves were free."

Liberty, he declares, is the cause of man ; but
he distrusted the patriotism of professed patriots
who were themselves the slaves of private passions, and whose universal philanthropy left
them indifferent to those humbler charities " for
whose dear sake their country, if at all, must be
beloved."

It is less by virtue of his ardor on behalf of
political liberty, genuine as that was, than by his
feeling for simplification and his humanitarian
sentiment that Cowper belongs to the Revolu-

tion. Mr. Leslie Stephen has described Cowper's
first independent volume of poems — that of
1782 — as "in substance a religious version of
Rousseau's denunciations of luxury.". It is, in
large measure, a restatement of the criticism of
society found in Brown's "Estimate of the Manners and Principles of the Age." Cowper had
retired from the world; he firmly believed in the
gains of retirement, though not of a hermit's solitude. From his retreat at Olney he observed the
world, and would fain play the part of a monitor
to his countrymen. Were he worthy to wear the
prophetic mantle, he would prophesy as well as
preach. It seemed to him that literature itself
was infected by the effeminacy of a luxurious age.
He had himself a very admirable gift for elegant
trifling in verse; but his conception of the func-
tion of poetry was lofty: that an eagle should
stoop from on high to pounce a wren, he held,
was hardly worthy of an aquiline spirit. He,
alas, was no eagle; yet he might achieve something towards the reform of poetry: first, by re-
covering simplicity and truth; secondly (but this,
he feared, was a task beyond his powers), by in-
fusing into it some of the true prophetic fervor
and insight; thirdly, by directing it towards a
new and lofty theme, that of religion. He was

sickened by the creamy smoothness of modern
song; his ear was fatigued by the "clockwork
tintinnabulum of rhyme;" he loved the vigorous
line that ploughs its stately course

"Like a proud swan, conquering the stream by force."

He conceived the poet at his highest, as a bard
who foresees the future in its moral causes, and
is deeply moved by his own vision : —

"A terrible sagacity informs
  The poet's heart, he looks to distant storms,
  He hears the thunder ere the tempest lowers,
  And, armed with strength surpassing human powers,
  Seizes events as yet unknown to man,
  And darts his soul into the dawning plan."

It were, indeed, something new in eighteenth-
century poetry, if such a bard — "a bard all
fire" — were to sing of the holiest theme with
lips touched by a coal from heaven.

Looking abroad from his retirement, Cowper
seemed to perceive that England was ailing at
the heart. He saw avarice, luxury, venality,
perjury, alike in Church and State. He pictures
Occidius, the fiddling priest, who, when he has
prayed and preached the Sabbath down, concludes the day with wire and catgut; and Rufil-
lus the elegant trifler, —

> " Exquisitely formed by rule,
> Not of the moral but the dancing school; "

and Gorgonius, the gourmand,

> " Abdominous and wan,
> Like a fat squab upon an Indian fan; "

and Petronius, whose original was Lord Chester-
field, —

> " Polished and finished foe to truth,
> Gray-beard corrupter of our listening youth.'

Like Brown, he laments the lack of discipline
at school and college, and the errors, vices, and
affectations acquired by the moneyed youth on
his grand tour of Europe. Learning in itself
is good, and wit is good, but what if both be
corrupt ? What if the salt have lost its savor ?
Happier, as he says in a well-known passage, the
poor cottager, weaving all day for a scanty pittance, and knowing no more than that her Bible
is true, than the Parisian demigod Voltaire, the
possessor of spirit, genius, and eloquence.

Cowper, in his recoil from the luxury and arti-
ficiality of eighteenth-century society, did not go
to the extremes in which Rousseau sometimes
indulged his morbid sensibility; he held that
civilized life is friendly to virtue, but not such
perverted civilization as is seen in modern cities,

— "God made the country, and man made the town ": —

> "Rank abundance breeds
> In gross and pampered cities, sloth and lust,
> And wantonness and gluttonous excess."

The varieties of evil are countless, — peculation, fraud, corruption, perjury, sale of honor, tricks, and lies; but of all these the source is one, — "profusion unrestrained," a hungry vice, which eats up all that gives society its beauty, strength, and use. Even the simplicity of rural life has been invaded; the country is no longer the Arcadia of Virgil or of Sidney, — "no, we are polished now;" fashion has travelled from the city streets to the village; the rustic beauty adorns her head with ribbons, and totters on high French heels; the ploughman follows the red-coats, and returns to his native cottage instructed how to swear, to game, to drink. Cowper feared that the whole course of human things was tending from good to ill and from ill to worse. Human nature left to itself appeared to Rousseau essentially beautiful and pure ; Cowper held a different creed, and he was no sharer in the optimism of the Revolution. The Second Book of "The Task" was named "The Time-Piece," because it was intended, as the author informed

Newton, to strike the hour that gives notice of approaching judgment.

Thus, although he was far from being a spirit of Revolution, Cowper mourns in Revolutionary fashion over the growth of luxury and the evils of a spurious civilization; thus he pleads for a return to simplicity of manners. He expresses no less clearly the humanitarian sentiment of the time. One of the pieces in his first volume is named "Charity;" the whole race of mankind, he maintains, constitutes a great fraternity; he contrasts the brotherly kindness of Captain Cook to his freeborn brethren of distant isles with the inhumanity of Cortez; he does honor to commerce, the providential purpose of which is to bind together land to land and race to race, but he reprobates with deep indignation the commerce in human flesh and blood, those cargoes of despair, against which Clarkson and Wilberforce pleaded; he celebrates the generous devotion of Howard in quitting rural peace for scenes of woe, and traversing Europe not to bring home the treasures of art but the knowledge that dungeons teach. In an age of humanity and sensibility the tender emotion naturally passed beyond the bounds of our own species, and spread over the whole animal creation. We re-

member how Cowper found a solace for his haunt-
ing grief in affection for his tame hares, Puss,
Tiny, and Bess.   In "The Task" he tells of his
delight in the happiness of the bounding fawn,
the horse's voluntary race, the uncouth gambol-
ling of cattle.   Prophet though Balaam was, he
might not without rebuke strike the blameless
ass on which he rode.   The poet would not
include in his list of friends, —

"Though graced with polished manners and fine sense,
  Yet wanting sensibility, the man
  Who needlessly sets foot upon a worm.
  An inadvertent step may crush the snail
  That crawls at evening in the public path;
  But he that has humanity, forewarned,
  Will tread aside, and let the reptile live."

The sentiment to which he gives utterance is
that which inspired Burns in his poem, "To a
Mouse on turning up her Nest with the Plough,"
and gave its moral —

> "He prayeth best who loveth best
> All things, both great and small " —

to Coleridge's "Ancient Mariner."   It is the
eighteenth-century sensibility united with the
Revolutionary sentiment of fraternity spreading
itself abroad over the whole animal world.

But though Cowper gives expression to the

Revolutionary feeling in favor of simplification and to the passion of human brotherhood, no one can imagine the poet of Olney, masculine as his spirit was, flinging himself with fury against the thrones of kings or the palaces of prelates. In political matters he desired not revolution but temperate reform. And with Cowper the circumference which rounded all subjects of thought and feeling, and towards which his mind constantly expanded, was the idea of God. If he reverenced truth, it was not in the spirit of those proud forerunners of the Revolution who did homage to human reason; he bowed the head and bowed the knee before what he deemed to be divine truth. If he spoke of equality, it was of the equality of all souls before the Supreme. The fraternity which he regarded as most perfect is the fraternity of those who are brethren in Christ. He invokes charity as the first and fairest of virtues, but he maintains that genuine charity is the offspring of divine instruction; we become sensible of our own poverty, our frailty, our deep disease, and so we learn pity for our fellows. He chooses Hope for his theme; but he has no vision of a terrestrial paradise to be realized by scientific progress or the overthrow of earthly tyrannies. It is from the very vanity of this world that our highest hope is born ; the whole creation groans and travails. But hope that is seen is not hope ; and the fulfilment shall be only when the Lord of earth shall descend, " propitious in his chariot paved with love." Cowper pleads for simplicity, for a return to nature ; but he adds that Nature of herself cannot restore to man the glories he has lost; to effect this, grace must come to the aid of Nature.

Thus the gospel of Rousseau is translated by Cowper into the gospel according to St. Paul. The combination is a curious and interesting one for literary study, of the sentiment of the Revolution with the faith and fervor of the Evangelical revival.

Were the village folk of England really threatened, as Cowper alleges, by the invasion of luxury ? A different report was made by one of his younger contemporaries who had himself known the life of the poor, and who had resolved to state nothing in verse that could not be verified to the letter. With the development of manufactures by machinery the domestic industries were perishing ; small farms were consolidated into larger properties which necessarily passed into the hands of the wealthy ; the small farmer became a day-laborer ; common lands

were enclosed; prices rose out of proportion to
the increase of wages. The transition of industry from the field and the cottage to the factory,
beneficial and inevitable as that transition was,
could not but be accompanied by much suffering
for the rural population, much demoralization for
the artisan. Within a year after the appearance
of Cowper's first volume was published a poem
which depicted with uncompromising realism the
life of the poor on the southeastern coast of
England, — "The Village," written by Crabbe,
read in manuscript by Burke, revised and
emended by Johnson. The romance of happy
swains and nymphs seemed to Crabbe to insult
the wretchedness of the peasant; he would declare the fact and nothing but the fact. He
describes the niggard sandy soil; the scanty
harvest beset with weeds; the wild amphibious
race, half peasants, half fishers, who gain more
by smuggling than by lawful dealings, bold, art-
ful, surly, savage. If they toil half-fed in the
fields, fevers and agues are their only certain
reward; a manhood of hopeless labor is followed by an old age of neglected misery. The
parish work-house is the refuge of despair,
where the happiest inhabitants are "the mop-
ing idiot and the madman gay." At last the

bitter day closes; the pauper's bier is borne to
the pauper's grave; the mourners follow, "se-
dately torpid and devoutly dumb;" the bell
tolls somewhat tardily; the priest has weightier
cares to engage him — a fox-hunt or a whist-
party — than the dull business of assisting at a
mendicant's funeral.

> " And waiting long, the crowd retire distrest
>   To think a poor man's bones should lie unblest."

Has Crabbe any consolation to offer, any
power to point to a bow of promise in the
clouds, or even any indignant cry for justice ?
He has none; the weight of misery oppresses
him; if the poor suffer, they have the vices
of the poor, and some of their misery is de-
served; only he would have the great ones of
the earth know that they are allied to their humbler fellows, if by nothing else at least by vice;
and the poor should learn that those whom they
envy are allied to them by hidden miseries hardly
less than theirs, though of another kind. The
age of patrons was not yet past; and "The Village" arrives at a most inappropriate and impo-
tent conclusion, with an eulogy of the virtue and
gallantry of a young sailor of the house of Rut-
land who had died in action with the French.

Crabbe sets forth with unfaltering fidelity the state of things which caused others to look upon the popular outbreak in France as the signal for a general revolt of the proletariat. But he does not dream of revolt; he will not be cheated by illusions; he thinks only of hopeless endurance.

II

THEORISTS OF REVOLUTION: GODWIN, MARY WOLLSTONECRAFT

II

THEORISTS OF REVOLUTION

THE doctrine of the Revolution was presented to English readers, not in immediate relation to politics, but in the way of philosophical speculation, more impressively than elsewhere in Godwin's "Enquiry concerning Political Justice" (1793). Occupying a position at some distance from the actual events of the French Revolution, Godwin could the more easily speculate on the theory of society. To do this was more easy for him than for a practical politician; but perhaps it was more dangerous, for the pressure of facts exercises a wholesome influence on speculation. Two great revolutions had taken place, — the uprising of the American colonies and the uprising against the French monarchy and the old régime. A thinker would naturally be led to consider the meaning of these vast phenomena. By the character of Godwin's mind, he was in a high degree qualified for the construction of a theory, and for the uncompromising application of ideas to life.

He was not a man of simple and warm feelings, — feelings which may serve to enrich a doctrine of life or to hold it in check; he was somewhat of a pedant among facts, chastising them into line and order to suit his rectilinear arrangement; a pedantic morality that reduces duty to a kind of geometry had more attraction for him than a morality that winds itself into the truths of human nature.   He had a certain haughtiness of intellect; he preferred the method of deduction from a general principle in morals and politics to the more modest method of induction.   His imagination was not wide-orbing and comprehensive, but it had considerable analytic power when applied to this point or to that.   He had a remarkable gift for imposing upon himself; he reverenced his own understanding, and profoundly believed that his character was that of a benevolent sage.   Such men as Godwin, narrowed in by a doctrinaire intellect, a contracted imagination, and the egoism of unwavering self-esteem, are dangerous.   They have in them the material for the making of fanatics.   It might be supposed that Godwin's coldness of temperament — a coldness which disappeared when his vanity was touched — would have saved him from fanaticism; but as there is a fiery fanaticism of the

passions, so there is a cold fanaticism of the idea.
At another time his cumbrous speculations might
have remained lifeless or inert; the genius of
Revolution gave them a vitality and energy which
were not properly their own. From the heart of
his icy doctrine there gleamed an iridescence of
extravagant hopes.

His influence with young and ardent spirits
was great. He seemed to provide a comprehensive theory of conduct, — a doctrine embracing
both private and public duties. This doctrine
was one which gave unbounded freedom to the
individual reason; the law was a proclamation of
liberty; moral anarchy was exhibited as the highest moral order. For a time Godwin's teaching
was accepted with characteristic ardor by Southey.
Coleridge submitted to the force of his reasonings,
but before long became a revolter. " Throw aside
your books of chemistry," said Wordsworth to a
student in the Temple, " and read Godwin on Necessity." A remarkable though a neglected poem
of Wordsworth, his early tragedy " The Borderers,"
marks the precise moment at which he recoiled
in alarm from the lessons of Godwin. In that
drama a generous youth is seduced into crime
through the sophistical reasoning of an elder man,
who by a specious abuse of the intellect dis-

integrates all natural feelings, all habitual moral checks, and would replace these by the unaided guidance of the private reason. It has been pointed out by M. Legouis, in his admirable study " La Jeunesse de William Wordsworth," that certain of the " Lyrical Ballads " in their vindication of the natural affections and the deep reverence with which they regard the permanent passions of humanity, furnish a reply and a rebuke to those doctrines of Godwin which had once dominated Wordsworth's mind. But if we would see the principles of the " Political Justice " translated into poetry and realized in action, we have only to study the writings and the life of his pupil and son-in-law, Shelley. Shelley, unlike Wordsworth and unlike Coleridge, was deficient in the power of original thought. Here, indeed, lies the capital infirmity of Shelley's genius. He accepted *en bloc* a system which, though doubtless it had affinities with his mind, was not the native growth of his intellect, — a system which was imposed upon him by a master. In M. Paul Bourget's novel " Le Disciple " the young hero of the story becomes the intellectual pupil of a scientific sage, a man of aspiring ideas and almost ascetic life, a saintly compounder of poisonous theory ; and by acting out the doctrine formulated by his master, but never by him tested in the stress of life nor carried fully into action, the disciple wrecks his whole existence, and inflicts irreparable injury on others. How far was the master responsible — such is M. Paul Bourget's problem — for the disciple's errors and crimes? The case of Shelley was not so unfortunate; his action upon the world has been, in the larger reckoning, beneficent; but it is demonstrable that many of the errors of his life and almost all the fallacies which lie behind the color and music of his art were directly due to his uncompromising discipleship to Godwin, together with that zeal which possessed Shelley for carrying immediately into practice those ideas which he accepted as true.

To form a just estimate of the concussion, as Godwin calls it, which the minds of men underwent through the impact of the Revolution, it is well to make acquaintance with " Political Justice " in the first edition. For later texts the first four books and the last book were in great part rewritten; variations are scattered everywhere throughout the books; and some of the most striking doctrinaire extravagances disappear. The design of Godwin's treatise was formed in May, 1791, when he was in his thirty-sixth year; and for sixteen months he devoted himself to his

task with the utmost ardor. Twelve years previously, as he informs his readers in the Preface,
he had become satisfied that monarchy is a species
of government essentially corrupt, — a conviction
which he derived not directly from observation,
but from books, in particular from the political
writings of Swift and from the Latin historians.
At the same time he was much influenced by the
works of the French philosophers of the eighteenth century, — by D'Holbach's "Système de la
Nature," the writings of Rousseau, and those of
Helvétius. The events of the French Revolution
convinced him of the evils of a complicated system of government; and by degrees he arrived
at the conclusion that government by its very
nature counteracts the improvement of the individual mind. His early faith in Providence and
in God had faded away; but it was from one
whose theological orthodoxy was pre-eminent,
from Jonathan Edwards, that he adopted certain of his arguments in favor of the philosophical
doctrine of necessity. Atheist, materialist, and
necessarian as at this time he was, no man ever
asserted more strongly the omnipotence of mind;
and it would be unjust to Godwin not to recognize the fact that, while sapping at the bases of
morality, he did so in the cause of what he con-

ceived to be a higher and stricter system of morals. His power of persuasion with young men of generous temper and speculative intellect is in itself an attestation of the magnanimous aspect which at the first view his system presented.

By the words Political Justice Godwin means the application of justice to society and to all its arrangements. But what is justice? It means the impartial treatment of every man in matters that relate to his happiness, and thus it may be said to comprise all moral duty. With Godwin politics is no mere affair of party expediency, but rather a department of the science of morals. In "Rasselas" Johnson makes his astronomer speak of the task of a king who has only the care of a few millions to whom he cannot do much good or harm. In a like spirit he conceived the lines which he contributed to the close of "The Traveller," —

"In every government, though terrors reign,
Though tyrant kings, or tyrant laws, restrain,
How small, of all that human hearts endure,
That part which laws or kings can cause or cure!"

"Sir," said Johnson to Adam Fergusson, "I would not give half a guinea to live under one form of government rather than another. It is of no moment to the happiness of an individual. Sir, the abuse of power is nothing to a private man. What Frenchman is prevented from passing his life as he pleases ?" Against this opinion, that the happiness of individuals is little affected by governments, Godwin justly and energetically protests. Millions of men in former ages were led to war under the standards of great conquerors, and they ravaged innumerable provinces. In domestic administration the established and approved methods of persuading the subject to obedience have been whips, axes, gibbets, dungeons, chains, racks: do not these somewhat disturb the happiness of the individual ? The moral characters of men are formed, according to Godwin, by the play of circumstance upon mind, and of all modes of acting upon mind he held that government is the most considerable. Fortunately human nature is capable of indefinite growth; man is not a perfect being, but he is perfectible; and among the causes that contribute to his moral improvement the most important are education, literature, and political justice. Vice and sin, as we understand these terms, have no real existence; vice, according to Godwin, is only an intellectual error, an erroneous perception, converted into action ; and on the other hand the

most essential part of virtue consists in endeavor-
ing to inform ourselves more accurately upon the
subject of utility and right.   Unhappily wide-
spread errors have been embodied and made permanent in the prevailing institutions of society;
and the tendency of every government is to
prompt us to seek the public welfare, not, as
should be the case, by means of innovation and
improvement, but in a timid reverence for the
decisions of our ancestors.   What has been the
result ?   What is the state of things as regards
human happiness that we see around us ?   In the
most refined countries of Europe, vast numbers of
the inhabitants are deprived of almost every
accommodation that can render life secure or even
tolerable.   The misery of the many is aggravated
by the ostentatious luxury, the magnificence, the
usurpation, the insolence of the fortunate few.
Nor is this a passing phase of society ; the un-
endurable evils are perpetuated by legislation,
which in almost every country grossly favors the
rich as against the poor, and by the iniquitous
administration of iniquitous laws.   Entire classes
of men are banded together to operate as organized bodies against social progress; priests, who
are accustomed on all occasions to have their
opinions listened to with deference, are inevita-

bly imperious, dogmatic, and impatient of opposition, and yet there exists a priestly caste; "their importance is connected with their real or supposed mental superiority over the rest of mankind; they *must* therefore be patrons of prejudice and implicit faith; their prosperity depends upon the reception of particular opinions in the world; they *must* therefore be enemies to freedom of inquiry."

And now, seeing such a world lying around us in error, what is justice? What is that moral principle which should be embodied in the institutions of society, and in every act of every one of its members? The principle of justice is this, — that each individual should do to others all the good that is in his power, and that society should do everything for its members that can contribute to their welfare. All personal and private feelings must be repressed and finally destroyed; family ties, special preferences, friendship, gratitude to benefactors are prejudices unworthy of an enlightened lover of his species. In distributing benefits among others I am bound to consider solely how they may be most conducive to the general good. Suppose the choice lay before me of rescuing from fire the author of the immortal "Telemachus," or my mother, my wife, or my child; who can question that the author of "Telemachus" is more likely to render important service to mankind? What magic is there in the pronoun *my?* My mother may be a fool; she may be malicious, mendacious, or dishonest. As for the superstition of gratitude, why should I suppose that I owe my benefactor a debt? He can have done no more than it was his duty to do. My own property and my own life I must equally hold in trust for others. The sole question that should determine conduct is this: How can I produce the greatest quantity of general good?

In place of the present system of inequality, with its distinctions of rank and class and wealth, political justice admits only natural inequalities: first, a certain physical superiority or inferiority, which, however, has been much exaggerated; and, secondly, the inequality of men's merits and virtues. A career should be left open to all talents; "we should endeavor to afford to all the same opportunities and the same encouragements, and to render justice the common interest and choice." Rights of man were pleaded for; Godwin, a stern moralist, acknowledges no such rights; man has only duties, or rather a single duty in all its varieties of application, that of

benefiting his fellows to the utmost. This is our
sole duty, and to ascertain the particulars of that
duty there is but one means, — the exercise of
the understanding. Hence, if we would make
other men virtuous, we can do so in no other way
than by enlightening and convincing their intellect. Racks, whips, and chains may disappear
forever. To punish a murderer is both unjust
and absurd ; and for two reasons, — in the first
place, he acted as he must of necessity have
acted, he had no more freedom than the knife
which he employed; and in the second place,
the gallows is an appeal to selfish fears and not
to the murderer's intelligence. Argue with him,
convince him of his erroneous estimate of happiness, and you have done all that you ought,
you have done all that you can.

The cultivation of truth, accordingly, is one
of the chief human duties. But in order that
we should ascertain truth, we must be constantly prepared to correct past errors, we must
perpetually revise our opinions in the light of
our new attainments. Hence the individual man
must guard against the sense of obligation to his
former self, and in like manner a nation ought
at every moment to be prepared to break with
its past. Each act of our individual lives, each

act of national life, ought to arise from an immediate perception of the truth, so far as at the
moment truth can be ascertained; nor should
any act of our former selves nor any national
act of our forefathers shackle or hamper our
freedom of the present hour. It necessarily
follows that promises and vows are in their very
nature immoral. They are needless, for every
instant prescribes its own duty, to which a
promise can add no authority. They are mis-
chievous, inasmuch as they substitute a fictitious
obligation derived from the past for the living
and immediate voice of reason. For a like reason
the obedience of one man to another or to a government partakes of the nature of immorality.
It deprives our reason of its sovereign prerogative. To justice and to truth we are bound to
submit, because they approve themselves to our
understanding; but in no case can we be bound
to submit to authority or to force. It were best
if society were permitted to develop itself without government of any kind, as a body of independent units, each subject to justice and to
reason, each, therefore, devoted to the good of all
the rest. But if a government be established,
let it, at least, be the simplest possible of governments in its necessary arrangements; and

that its action may be free and intelligent, let every member of the community have a share in its formation. Thus only can each man be inspired by a consciousness of his own importance, and "the slavish feelings that shrink up the soul in the presence of an imagined superior" cease to exist. At any moment it may become a duty to resist the government and effect a revolution. But Godwin maintained that physical violence is unworthy of a rational being; revolutions are to be conducted by means of argument and persuasion. The best security for an advantageous issue to a revolutionary movement lies in free and complete discussion of individual with individual. Anything of the nature of political associations is to be feared as tending to tumult and unreason.

So Godwin, with a kind of implacable idealism, erected his fabric of political justice. This he did, not as one who would construct an imaginary commonwealth, or picture an Utopia. He was possessed by an ardent faith in his own ideas as about to be realized, by an unquenchable hope in the future of mankind. The keystone of his entire structure he held to be a genuine system of property. To whom, he asks, does any article of property, suppose a loaf of bread, justly belong ? Assuredly to him who wants it most, or to whom the possession of it will be most beneficial. Every man is entitled, so far as the general stock will suffice, not only to the means of being but of well-being. Every man should make his contribution to the common stock, and every man should possess his share. Religious teachers have indeed urged upon their disciples the practice of charity ; but they have represented charity as an affair of spontaneous generosity, a species of bounty ; whereas the distribution of every shilling that we possess is in truth a mere act of justice. " Religion," adds Godwin, " is in reality in all its parts an accommodation to the prejudices and weaknesses of mankind." He calculates that half an hour out of each day employed in manual labor by every member of the community would sufficiently supply the whole with necessaries. Let it not be supposed, however, that Godwin was of the school of modern socialism. On the contrary, he is an uncompromising individualist. Everything of the nature of co-operation was repellent to his mind. He even anticipated the time when a musical concert in which several performers take part will be felt to be an intolerable anomaly ; and when, for truly rational auditors, a solitary musician will perform the whole, rendering his own compositions, since no other than his own can be native to his reason and his imagination; a time when theatrical exhibitions must cease, because no human being in the age of enlightenment will come forward to repeat ideas and words that are not his own. In that happier epoch, moreover, man and woman will co-operate as husband and wife only for so long as each may deem it beneficial. The institution of marriage is "a system of fraud;" it is "law and the worst of laws;" it is a violation of individual liberty, — the engrossing of one human being by another. The family, as we know it, will merge itself in the universal family of mankind. Each human unit being independent, yet bound to every other human unit by justice, Godwin expected that at no distant date surnames would pass out of use; man will at last be man, no less and no more, —

> "Sceptreless, free, uncircumscribed, but man
> Equal, unclassed, tribeless, and nationless,
> Exempt from awe, worship, degree, the king
> Over himself; just, gentle, wise."

As mind advances in its mastery over matter, it may well be that the secret of terrestrial immortality shall be discovered. The immortals of earth, with their improved understandings, will perceive the evil consequences of multiplying the population. In that golden age of reason all men will be adults ; the existence of children will be known only by the records of ancient history. There will then be no crimes, no bolts or bars, no enforced obedience, no gratitude, no sentiment of the family, no love of country, no administration of justice (as it is called), and no government. " These latter articles," writes Godwin, " are at no great distance ; and it is not impossible that some of the present race of men may live to see them in part accomplished. But beside this, there will be no disease, no anguish, no melancholy, and no resentment. Every man will seek with ineffable ardor the good of all." Is it to Godwin or to Shelley that we are listening ? It is indeed to both, for the disciple in his more doctrinaire poems only translated into terms of emotion and imagination the intellectual oracles of the master.

" He is a dreamer ; let us leave him ; pass." And pass we might, save for two reasons : First, Godwin, and Shelley with him, if dreamers, dreamed a portion of the truth ; fragments of the dream were prophetic of actual tendencies in modern society. That is one reason why it is worth attending to the voice that speaks in "Political Justice." And the second reason is that the book, with all its fantastic illusions, is in a high degree representative of the time. Its utilitarian ethics are the ethics of the second half of the eighteenth century; the reigning personage of the treatise is the revolutionary abstraction, — Man; man, denuded of all distinctions, viewed apart from all conditions and circumstances. The three sacred words of the Revolution — liberty, equality, fraternity — are adopted and written large by Godwin: liberty the most absolute; equality as complete as can be attained, for certain natural inequalities the theorist is unable to deny; fraternity, realized in principles of universal benevolence. The whole body of Godwin's thought is inspired by that boundless faith in human nature which sustained and animated the nobler spirits of 1789; human perfectibility is a cardinal article in his creed; his hopes for the future are as assured as they are extravagant. The worship of Reason is celebrated in the system of the philosopher with the pious orgies of a frigid enthusiasm. "Mankind," says Mr. Leslie Stephen, "is, or ought to be, in Godwin's view a vast collection of incarnate syllogisms." Godwin's conception is of something yet more for-

midable; every incarnate syllogism is, or ought
to be, possessed by the zeal of an aggressive benevolence. Happily each is isolated; each human
intelligence is a single, separate entity.   No
writer expresses more clearly than Godwin the
individualism of the opening of the Revolutionary
movement of Europe.   Nor does any writer exhibit more strikingly its entire lack of historical
thought and feeling.   Man is not conceived as
growing out of the past; the heritage from former generations is a heritage of superstition,
tyranny, unreason; it exists only to be relin-
quished or destroyed. The Year One has arrived;
and the whole world is to be reconstructed, without reference to inheritance or accumulated tendencies, on the principles of the Reason.   There is
something sublime, something pathetic, something
ludicrous in the heroic folly with which the philosopher in his study calmly remodels the entire
world of humanity.   But the fallacies as well as
the truths of "Political Justice" belong less to
the individual writer than to the extraordinary
epoch in the world's history in which he lived
and moved.

The "Enquiry concerning Political Justice"
was published in February, 1793.   "In this year
also," says Godwin, "I wrote the principal part

of the novel of 'Caleb Williams,' which may perhaps be considered as affording no inadequate image of the fervor of my spirit; it was the off-spring of that temper of mind in which the composition of my 'Political Justice' left me." In "Caleb Williams" we have before us a revolutionary work of art, the imaginative work of a theorist, a tale which enforces a doctrine. It gains and loses by the concentration of spirit with which Godwin in it studies and works out a moral problem. To read it is to enter and explore a cavern; it is narrow; it is dark; we lose the light and air, and the clear spaces of the firmament; but the explorer's passion seizes upon us, and we grope along the narrowing walls with an intensity of curious desire. As the work of a political thinker, the book is an indictment of society. "Things as they are" — this, and not the name of the hero — is the first title of Godwin's novel; and things as they are present themselves to the reader as, in the main, things as they ought not to be. The gentry of England are exhibited under two types. Mr. Falkland, a gentleman sensitive, refined, benevolent, possessed by all the sentiments of a romantic chivalry, is brought into antagonism with a brutal and over-bearing country squire. He opposes himself with firm yet gentle magnanimity to Tyrrel's acts of tyrannic injustice; at length, in the whirl of passion following an outrageous insult, Falkland stabs to death his antagonist. The thought of making his own exit from the world on the gallows with a dishonored name is intolerable to his sense of aristocratic dignity. He permits two innocent rustics, a father and a son, who are suspected of the murder, to bear the penalty of his crime; and forever after he is haunted by remorse, afflicted by sudden spasms of anguish and of shame, while to counterbalance his evil deed he devotes his life to the service of his fellows. Mr. Falkland's young secretary, Caleb Williams, drawn on by the very enthusiasm of curiosity, dominated by a passion to probe the mysteries of the human spirit, penetrates to the dreadful secret of his master's guilt, and thenceforth becomes the victim of a persecution which is unfaltering so far as it is essential to the preservation of Falkland's fair fame, and yet is unstained by the baseness of personal malignity. Falkland dies in the agony and blessed relief of a public confession of his crime.

Godwin's ambition as a thinker and a man of letters was arduous and lofty. The most characteristic features of his mind in childhood, he tells us, were religion and a love of distinction. His religious zeal transformed itself into political enthusiasm; his love of distinction remained, and took the form of literary ambition. During ten years he had toiled without success. "Everything I wrote," he says in the preface to "Fleetwood," "fell still-born from the press." At length, with the publication of "Political Justice," fame arrived, and with it came an enhanced sense of power. He had always believed that he possessed the gifts of an inventor of fictitious narrative, and in setting to his task he repeated to himself, again and again, the words: "I will write a tale that shall constitute an epoch in the mind of the reader, and no one, after he has read it, shall ever be exactly the same man that he was before." "Caleb Williams" is indeed a product of the will, — a work of strenuous resolve rather than the offspring of genial creation. The writer first constructed a problem, and then set himself to unravel its difficulties. He began by thinking out the close of his story, and then worked backward from the catastrophe to its causes; having formed the plan of his third volume, he proceeded as it were along necessary lines of causation to the second volume, and from that again to the first. There is a strong concatenation of

plot interest, and the characters are constructed
to support and expound the plot; but in a work
so calculated we miss the joy which comes with
a sense of free imaginative growth. Godwin
wrote in the first person, after having tried the
more usual way of narrative, because it suited
better his purpose of analysis, and guided what
he terms his "metaphysical dissecting-knife" in
tracing and laying bare the involutions of motive.
He planted himself at his desk only when his
theme possessed him, laying aside his manuscript
for days or weeks when he was not fully in the
vein. "Idleness was only time lost . . .; it was
merely a day perished from the calendar. But a
passage written feebly, flatly, or in the wrong
spirit constituted an obstacle that it was next to
impossible to correct and set right again." Thus
for twelve months he lived during his best hours
in his realm of invention, and then his task was
achieved.

To understand aright the motives of Godwin's
novel, it is necessary to collate the book with his
other writings. A preface to the first edition,
dated May 12, 1794, was withdrawn in compli-
ance with the bookseller's alarms; it appeared,
when the second edition was published, towards
the close of the following year. The acquittal

of Hardy and Horne Tooke, on the charge of
high treason, in the autumn of 1794, was taken
to indicate the collapse of what Godwin styles
" a sanguinary plot against the liberties of Englishmen." In his preface to "Caleb Williams," the
author explains his design of showing how "the
spirit and character of the government intrudes
itself into every rank of society." Representing
" things as they are," he is compelled to exhibit
the various modes of "domestic and unrecorded
despotism by which man becomes the destroyer
of man." The fatal error of Godwin's hero, Falkland, — an error maintained through life, and
only abandoned at the moment of death, — proceeds from his acceptance of a false standard
of morals; his is the aristocratic, the chivalric,
the traditional standard; he wrongs his nature
as a man, his humanity, in order to preserve
unstained his reputation as a gentleman and a
man of honor. In Tyrrel is presented the dulness, the grossness, the overbearing self-will, the
boisterous arrogance of one who possesses power
and position, not through desert, but merely by
inheritance. He is an oppressive landlord, who
does not scruple to ruin the industrious tenant;
a domineering head of a house, who would force
his brute will upon his dependants. Falkland is

made of finer metal; he is shocked by his rival's coarseness of feeling and perception; he actively opposes the tyranny of this rude lord of many acres. But Falkland is himself tainted by a subtler pride of rank and class, and when he suffers physical violence at the hands of his brawny antagonist all his blood turns to flame. Instead of recognizing, in a philosophic spirit, that no real dishonor could lie in the fact that his muscles are less powerful than those of a giant, he loses all sense of the truth of things, and sweeps on the instant to his revenge. That he may still live in the eyes and the memories of his fellows as a loyal gentleman, his whole existence becomes a lie. He is at once the culprit and the martyr of the chivalric ideal.

With the resources of wealth and influence at his command, it is easy for Falkland, under the forms of English law, to make his secretary the victim of legalized injustice. On a false accusation, Caleb Williams is thrown into prison, and long lies awaiting his trial, punished by a weary captivity before he has been convicted. "Thank God, exclaims the Englishman, we have no Bastille! Thank God, with us no man can be punished without a crime! Unthinking wretch! Is that a country of liberty where thousands languish in dungeons and fetters? Go, go, ignorant fool! and visit the scenes of our prisons! Witness their unwholesomeness, their filth, the tyranny of their governors, the misery of their inmates! After that show me the man shameless enough to triumph, and say, England has no Bastille! Is there any charge so frivolous upon which men are not consigned to these detested abodes? Is there any villany that is not practised by justices and prosecutors? But against all this, perhaps you have been told, there is a redress. Yes, a redress that it is the consummation of insult so much as to name! Where shall the poor wretch reduced to the last despair, and to whom acquittal perhaps comes just in time enough to save him from perishing, — where shall this man find leisure, and, much less, money, to fee counsel and officers, and purchase the tedious dear-bought remedy of the law? No, he is too happy to leave his dungeon, and the memory of his dungeon, behind him; and the same tyranny and wanton oppression become the inheritance of his successor." Naturally, if law was tyranny, the offenders, or alleged offenders, against the law were amiable and admirable victims of its evil sway. Godwin, confident in his own originality as a writer, did not fear to make studies for

"Caleb Williams" from the writings of former
authors, — from "The Adventures of Mademoi-
selle de Saint Phale," a French Protestant of
the times of the Huguenot persecutions, from
that tremendous compilation "God's Revenge
against Murther," from the "Lives of the Pirates." In the "Newgate Calendar" he found
an incident which he adapted to the purpose of
his novel. The ministers of the law are venal
tyrants; but among his fellow-prisoners Caleb
finds a young soldier of a most engaging countenance and a character distinguished by integrity
and refinement, who has been committed on a
false accusation of highway robbery. "His habits of thinking were peculiar, full of justice, simplicity, and wisdom." His favorite solace was
derived from the works of Horace and Virgil.
He spoke without bitterness of the injustice
under which he suffered, and predicted that the
time would come — but such happiness was reserved for posterity — when the possibility of
such intolerable oppression would be extirpated.
Brightwel, the young soldier, dies in prison, and
Caleb Williams receives his parting breath.

Escaped from confinement, Caleb secures for a
time an asylum in the lurking-place of a band of
robbers, and among these he discovers virtues

unknown to the men whose business it was to administer the laws of his country, that is, to wrest those laws to the advantage of the wealthy and the powerful.   At least these freebooters knew the joys of freedom : "they could form plans and execute them ; they consulted their own inclinations; they did not impose upon themselves the task, as is too often the case in human society, of seeming tacitly to approve that from which they suffered most ; or, which is worse, of persuading themselves that all the wrongs they suffered were right; but were at open war with their oppressors."   Among them were to be found benevolence and comradeship ; they were strongly susceptible of emotions of generosity.   They had no part in "the debilitating routine of human affairs ;" and hence they frequently displayed "an energy which from every impartial observer would have extorted veneration."   That it was a misapplied energy Godwin admits ; but energy, as such, is "perhaps of all qualities the most valuable."

Godwin's benevolent and venerable highwaymen stand in the moral scale far above the servile tribes of lawyers and parsons ; but they fall short of his ideal of manhood.   This ideal is indicated in his outline sketch of Mr. Collins, the steward of

Falkland's estate. Mr. Collins had befriended Caleb Williams in early youth as his father's executor. Almost to the end he remains convinced of his master's innocence, and believes that Caleb is guilty of the crimes laid to his charge. He is instructed in a mild and enlightened philosophy, and when he speaks, his words sound like a paragraph from "Political Justice." In that treatise Godwin had pushed to its furthest consequences the doctrine of necessity; there is no such thing as freedom of the will; therefore no indignation against wrong-doing (unless, perhaps, the tyranny of rulers and the frauds of priests) can be reasonable. All vice is merely error, a miscalculation of consequences. The murderer is no more to be detested than is the knife with which he perpetrated the murder. Mr. Collins has banished from his enlightened understanding the very ideas of crime and guilt. "You know," he says to Caleb, "my habits of thinking. I regard you as vicious; but I do not consider the vicious as proper objects of indignation and scorn. I consider you as a machine: you are not constituted, I am afraid, to be greatly useful to your fellow-men; but you did not make yourself; you are just what circumstances irresistibly compelled you to be. I am sorry for your ill properties;

but I entertain no enmity against you, nothing but benevolence. Considering you in the light in which I at present consider you, I am ready to contribute everything in my power to your real advantage, and would gladly assist you, if I knew how, in detecting and extirpating the errors that have misled you." So philosophizes the sage in presence of the unhappy youth, and no benevolent machine could creak out pedantic morals with more mechanical precision. Too evidently, among Godwin's gifts a sense of humor was not the most considerable.

" Caleb Williams " is the one novel of the days of Revolution, embodying the new doctrine of the time, which can be said to survive. No power of evocation can reanimate the forms which once moved as men and women through the tales of Holcroft and of Bage. Holcroft's " Memoirs," written in part by himself and continued to his death by Hazlitt, are indeed a piece of veritable life, a genuine record of heroism in literature. The child of a London shoemaker, whose wife sold greens and oysters, Holcroft came early to know the hardships and injuries of the poor. He tramped the country, hawking peddlery with his mother; he begged alms from the passers-by. He had risen in the world when as a stable-boy he groomed horses at Newmarket. In his pages we are on terms of pleasant intimacy with famous racers and jockeys whose moments of triumph are more than a century gone by. Between stable hours he learnt the rule of three, and, with an old nail for pencil, cast up sums on the paling of the stable-yard. In due time he set up a country school, had one scholar, and lived on potatoes and buttermilk. As a poor player he appeared in Macklin's company and trod the boards of Dublin theatres. From actor he climbed to author, writing many pieces for the stage which are now forgotten, and one, " The Road to Ruin," which has some claim to be remembered. In 1784 he was attracted to Paris by the celebrity of Beaumarchais' "Marriage of Figaro," — that drama which caught the colors of the Revolutionary dawn before the sun had risen. With the assistance of a friend Holcroft transcribed the play from the recollection of successive performances ; he adapted it to the English stage, himself acted the part of Figaro, and received an ample reward from the theatre. Sprung from the people, and acquainted with the lot of the poor, ardent and aspiring of temper, he became a zealot for the principles of the French Revolution, and was indicted with Hardy and his companions for high treason. In his novel "Anna St. Ives" he creates his personages — so Hazlitt cannot but admit — as the vehicles of certain general sentiments, or "machines put into action," with a view to reducing those sentiments to the supposed test of imagined action. Deeply stirred as Hazlitt himself was by the passions of the movement in France, he was too true in his feeling for literature to admire the pitiful drapery in which Holcroft clothes his political abstractions, in order that, "petticoated, booted, and spurred," they may show their paces on the high horse. "Hugh Trevor," which may be regarded as a sequel to "Anna St. Ives," aims at presenting a view of things as they are, of society with its decaying and demoralizing institutions, from which misery and vice are spread abroad as by some pestilential miasma. Holcroft's indictment of the established order in the pages of his novel is forgotten, but we still remember those verses of his which tell of the cold comfort offered to Gaffer Gray in the bitter January weather by parson, squire, and lawyer; it is only the poor man — so concludes the song — who can feel for the misery of the poor, and share his morsel with a fellow-sufferer.

Three of the novels of Robert Bage had the distinction of being included by Scott in Ballantyne's Novelist's Library. A Quaker by his education, Bage found his way to free thought in religion and in politics. His period of authorship began late in his life. He was fifty-three when " Mount Henneth," his first novel, was published ; other tales followed, and were well received ; and to the days of Revolution belong two with significant and contrasted titles, — " Man as he is " (1792), and " Hermsprong ; or, Man as he is not " (1796). In private life Bage was mild, amiable, temperate ; he reserved his audacities for the field of opinion on affairs of general interest, and those audacities proceeded in part from his ardent benevolence. Scott is generous in recognition of Bage's literary gifts, his quaint, facetious, ironical style, his truly English vein of humor ; but for his own part, Scott was not disposed to regard every person of superior rank and station as the wicked giant of a chivalric romance, nor every poor man as a being composed of virtue and generosity. The misrepresentation of the different classes of society was not the only error of Bage's novels ; Scott could not approve of their dangerous tendency to slacken the reins of discipline in the matter of the relation of the sexes. In the Revolutionary " return to nature," external law, custom, and tradition were treated as oppo-

nents rather than regulators of the impulses of
the heart and the dictates of the individual reason: "Hermsprong, whom Mr. Bage produces as
the ideal perfection of humanity, is paraded as a
man who, freed from all the nurse and all the
priest has taught, steps forward on his path,
without any religious or political restraint, as one
who derives his own rules of conduct from his
own breast, and avoids or resists all temptations
of evil passions, because his reason teaches him
they are attended by evil consequences." It is
the doctrine of Godwin transferred to the world
of imaginative creation; the doctrine which
Wordsworth had once embraced with ardor, and
from which he afterwards recoiled in alarm:

> "What delight!
> How glorious! in self-knowledge and self-rule,
> To look through all the frailties of the world,
> And, with a resolute mastery shaking off
> Infirmities of nature, time, and place,
> Build social upon personal Liberty,
> Which, to the blind restraints of general laws
> Superior, magisterially adopts
> One guide, the light of circumstances, flashed
> Upon an independent intellect."[1]

The reader of Bage's novels should compare
— so Scott suggests — his philosophic heroes

---

[1] The Prelude, book xi. ll. 235-244.

with the philosophic Square of Fielding's "Tom Jones," and consider seriously "whether a system of Ethics, founding an exclusive and paramount court in a man's own bosom for the regulation of his own conduct, is likely to form a noble, enlightened, and generous character . . . or whether it is not more likely, as in the observer of the rule of right, to regulate morals according to temptation and to convenience, and to form a selfish sophistical hypocrite, who, with morality always in his mouth, finds a perpetual apology for evading the practice of abstinence, when either passion or interest solicit him to indulgence." We cannot expect to perceive the results of a new code of ethics or a new principle of conduct until a generation springs up with which it has become a formative power; even then its full effect is held in check by a surrounding or intermingling part of society which still accepts the traditional standards. Happily the Revolutionary body of doctrine set forth in "Political Justice" was never fully tested in actual life. Some of its consequences when put in action appear in the errors of the youthful Shelley, — errors in which something of noble aspiring and devotion to an idea was mingled with unwarranted self-confidence and passionate self-will.

The calamities which almost overwhelmed
Godwin's first wife are in like manner directly
traceable to the new ethics of the time playing
upon an enterprising understanding and an impulsive sensitive heart. "As for panegyric,"
wrote Southey to a friend in 1801, "I never
yet praised living being except Mary Wollstonecraft." "She was a delightful woman," he wrote
to Caroline Bowles, a quarter of a century later,
"and in better times, or in better hands, would
have been an excellent one. But her lot had
fallen in evil days, and the men to whom she
attached herself were utterly unworthy of her.
. . . Few persons but those who have lived in it
can conceive or comprehend what the memory of
the French Revolution was, nor what a visionary world seemed to open upon those who were
just entering it. Old things seemed passing
away, and nothing was dreamt of but the re-
generation of the human race." The title of
Mary Wollstonecraft's best-known work, "A
Vindication of the Rights of Woman," has suggested to many persons a misconception of her
personal character and of the nature of her writings. She was, before all else, an ardent, sensitive human being, needing more than anything
else to love and to be loved. But she feared,

and with good reason, her own eager, craving, intemperate heart; she set her brain to work as a sentinel over that heart; but some of her intellectual conclusions only encouraged the audacity of her emotions. She speaks in "The Rights of Woman" of that "sanguine ardor which it has been the business of my life to depress." If we would study the emotional side of her nature, we must turn to the "Letters to Imlay," some of which are exquisite with strokes of genius prompted by the affections. Her treatise on the Rights of Woman was written with urgent speed, not merely to assert and maintain the claims which she made in favor of half the human race; it was written also to assert for her own benefit, and as it were against her own emotional temperament, the claims of reason. Her plea is not a plea for woman as against man, but for woman as against the sensual and the sentimental estimate of many men, and at the same time as against that part of her own sex which accepted and turned to their account this unworthy estimate. Her conception of the ideal woman was neither that of the doll of the doll's house, nor that of the chivalric queen of the court of love, nor that of the Eastern odalisque. It approached very near to the ideal of Wordsworth's lines, —

> " A Being breathing thoughtful breath,
> A Traveller between life and death ;
> The reason firm, the temperate will,
> Endurance, foresight, strength, and skill."

With such an ideal in view, Mary Wollstone-craft's book became in large part a pleading on behalf of a more serious and enlightened education for women. At the basis of all lay a sincere piety ; she maintained that woman holds her prerogative direct from God, and can accomplish her complete tasks only in a life immortal. On a groundwork of religion she would have a structure established of reason, self-control, and good sense. Such is the teaching of the book, though its lessons are often enfeebled by intemperate utterances, by crude rhetoric, and a want of becoming reserve. It is representative of the writer in its eagerness, its passionate accent ; it is no less representative of her in its effort to place reason above passion, not to suppress passion, but as a controlling and regulative principle. While thus expressing the mind and the temperament of an individual, " The Rights of Woman " is also essentially a document of the Revolutionary period. The Revolution professed itself to be an assertion of the reason in opposition to custom, prescription, tradition ; such also is the profession made in Mary Wollstonecraft's "Vindication." The Revolution treated with scorn the chivalric ideals; Mary Wollstonecraft's protest is vehement and repeated against the chivalric sentiment, its woman-worship springing from over-strained gallantry, its romantic exaltations which she takes to be only a rarified form of the creeping mists of sensuality. "It is not," she says, "against strong persevering passions, but romantic, wavering feelings, that I wish to guard the female heart by exercising the understanding." She admits that in the order of nature or of Providence enthusiastic illusions play a part in education; only through the exercise of human passions, she declares, can the lesson of life be fully learnt. But she would have the weight of the passions balanced by the weight of reason and a temperate will.

Ardent admirer of Rousseau, the prophet of Revolution, as Mary Wollstonecraft was, she strenuously set herself to oppose his teaching as far as it related to the position of her own sex and the education of women. While in the education of his Emilius Rousseau thinks primarily of the human virtues, in the education and training of his Sophia he thinks especially of the qualities of her sex. Woman is to be formed, not in order that she may be an admirable human being, but that she may attract and gratify man, her master. "We are confronted," as Mr. Morley puts it, "with the Oriental conception of woman. Every principle which has been followed in the education of Emilius is reversed in the education of women. Opinion, which is the tomb of virtue among men, is among women its high throne. The whole education of women ought to be relative to men; to please them, to be useful to them, to make themselves loved and honored by them, to console them, to render their lives agreeable and sweet to them, — these are the duties which ought to be taught to women from their childhood." Against such an ideal Mary Wollstonecraft protested with all the vehemence of her nature. She would have woman honored and honorable as a human creature, and pleasing to man as a comrade and a helpmate, not as a flatterer, a subject, or a slave.

Having set forth her general principles in "A Vindication of the Rights of Woman," Mary Wollstonecraft attempted to give imaginative embodiment to her convictions in a novel. The unfinished "Wrongs of Woman; or, Maria," bears a relation to the "Vindication" resembling that which "Caleb Williams" bears to "Political

Justice;" but bitter personal experiences and memories of her kinsfolk and her friends inflamed the spirit of Mary, and gave a character to her tale which contrasts strongly with the calculated logic of her husband's memorable work. The heroine, Maria, is the victim of a miserable marriage; she flies from her husband, but is seized by him, is separated from her child, and thrown, on the alleged ground of her lunacy, into a madhouse. Deluded by the ardor of her own heart, she escapes from captivity with a man who is unworthy of her; she is deserted by him, makes an attempt upon her life (but not in the precise manner of the narrator when abandoned by Imlay), recovers, and resolves to live for her child. The writer's main object, as stated in her Preface, is to exhibit the misery and oppression peculiar to women, that arise out of the partial laws and customs of society. It is a bitter cry of woman against the injuries of men, and as a statement of one side of the case by an advocate it had perhaps a certain value. The movement of society has to some extent justified the remonstrances of Mary Wollstonecraft; under the present law of England, her heroine, if art were life, could doubtless obtain a divorce from her domestic tyrant on the grounds of infidelity and cruelty.

Unfortunately, Mary Wollstonecraft's genius was little suited to continuous narrative; the story is repulsive without being powerful. The lecturer on moral ulcers should possess something of the scientific spirit; to pluck away the bandage, to expose the naked horror, and to declaim violently may not assist a cure; it may confuse and revolt the intelligence and even the senses of the witnesses. Possibly a female physician is not always the most judicious adviser in the moral maladies of her sex. The book, however, may be considered not as the physician's advice, but as a patient's statement of her case, or rather as the patient's cry of agony, wrung from her by intolerable pain. That cry is heard often in real life; to transfer its poignancy to art needs more self-restraint and higher imaginative gifts than were possessed by Mary Wollstonecraft.

NOTE.

Mary Wollstonecraft's experiment in philosophical history, " An Historical and Moral View of the Origin and Progress of the French Revolution ; and the Effect it has produced in Europe " (1794, first volume, all published), was an attempt beyond her powers, yet it may still be read with interest. In full view of the disasters and crimes of the Revolution, her optimism is unshaken. It is an optimism founded on a faith in the salutary effects of the advance of political enlightenment ; the crimes were crimes of passion, natural to a time of violent convulsion ;

the gains are gains of the reason, and are therefore of permanent and increasing worth.

More than one novel was written with the design of confuting Godwin's principles by exhibiting the consequences to which they lead. The best remembered, or the least forgotten, of these is "Edmund Oliver," dedicated to Charles Lamb, by his friend Charles Lloyd. The reproduction in fiction of some of S. T. Coleridge's early adventures has given the book an interest which its literary merits in themselves fail to justify. The heroine, Lady Gertrude Sinclair, is a disciple of "Political Justice," and at the same time a representative of the passionate sensibility admired and cultivated in the second half of the eighteenth century.

Among contemporary criticisms of "Political Justice" one of the ablest is "An Examination of the Leading Principle of the New System of Morals" (1798), an anonymous pamphlet by Thomas Green, who is best remembered as the author of the "Diary of a Lover of Literature." The argument of the writer is directed to prove that although the general good, utility, the happiness of the greatest number, may be the final cause of all virtuous action, it is not therefore the proximate cause. We act from many legitimate motives; to act from these motives tends to the general good; but to attempt a calculation of all the results of our action, and to regard the general good as our sole legitimate motive, would be to lose all capacity for action in the calculation of consequences. The reply to Godwin includes a reply to Paley.

III

ANTI-REVOLUTION: EDMUND BURKE

III

ANTI-REVOLUTION: EDMUND BURKE

In one of the most remarkable of Burke's later writings, his " Letter to a Noble Lord," he pleads for the repose due to old age, and in doing so he expresses himself in one of those violent images with which he was accustomed to relieve his overwrought feelings. " Why," he asks, " will they not let me remain in obscurity and inaction? Are they apprehensive that if an atom of me remains, the sect has something to fear? Must I be annihilated, lest, like old John Zisca's, my skin might be made into a drum, to animate Europe to eternal battle against a tyranny that threatens to overwhelm all Europe and all the human race?" No one at the present day can desire to convert Edmund Burke's skin into a drum on which to beat an anti-revolutionary tattoo. The time is past for that kind of polemical criticism; it is nearly a century since the words which have been quoted were written. The subject of our inquiry is literature; it is as a part of literature, in the larger sense of that word, that Burke's political writings must here be considered. 1 desire to contribute something towards the study of a great mind, a great nature and character, as affected by the most important events of the time. And as we have seen how a different type of mind, the doctrinaire type, was affected, in the example of William Godwin, so it will be worth observing how a mind fed by concrete fact, an understanding enlarged and sustained by great affairs, and a heart alive with every generous passion, were moved. The interest of the study will perhaps be rather psychological than political. Whether Burke help us to understand the Revolution or not, assuredly the Revolution should help us to understand Burke.

In a well-known canon of style Burke lays it down that the master sentence of every paragraph should involve, first, a thought, secondly, an image, and, thirdly, a sentiment. The rule is certainly not one of universal application; it is one not always followed by Burke himself, but it expresses the character of his mind. A thought, an image, a sentiment, and all bearing upon action,— it gives us an intimation that the writer who set forth such a canon was a com-

plete nature, no fragment of a man, but a full-
formed human spirit, and that when he came
to write or speak, he put his total manhood into
his utterance. This is, indeed, Burke's first and
highest distinction. He was deficient in none of
the parts or passions of a man; all were large
and vigorous, — judgment, affections, imagination,
will, — and each played into and through the
others. He did not isolate one province or section
of his nature for the uses of authorship; he did
not say, in Godwin's manner, "Go to, I will not
declare myself as pure and disembodied Reason; "
when he wrote, what guided his pen was nothing less than the whole man. And when Burke
looked abroad he saw the organism of society at
large, formed as it were on the same pattern as
that on which he himself was formed; he saw
reason, passions, imagination, will, native instincts,
and inherited customs, and all these alive and in
a state of mutual interaction. These, and much
besides, helped to constitute society. He felt
that unless he entered into sympathy with all of
these he could utter no adequate word. It is
related of Napoleon that when he had seen and
conversed with Goethe, the exclamation broke
from him, "There is a *man!*" The same expression involuntarily rises to our lips when we have

remained for a time in the presence of Edmund
Burke.

And this great nature had been formed and
developed amid great affairs. Burke was no
closet philosopher. He had lived and moved
among the eminent figures of his time. He had
become an important member of a powerful
political party. He had a share in the rise and
fall of ministries. He had an interest in a great
people, and cherished all its gains acquired
through the centuries. He was one with the
nation of England. Of the life of two continents
— of three continents, Europe, America, Asia, he
was a part. Such a man, so trained, could never
be a mere pedant; he could not be the oracle of
a coterie; he could not be the prophet or philosopher of a sect. At the least one entire side of
truth must find a voice when he spoke. His
writings form a broad stream into which many
affluents flowed; as it has been happily expressed,
they " drain a large area."

The position from which Burke viewed affairs
was the most fortunate position for the attain-
ment of practical wisdom. He did not forever
creep through the by-ways of petty detail; he
did not soar into the clouds of glittering generalities. His feet were on the substantial earth ;

but they were upon the heights, from which he gained a large prospect, and saw things in their broad relations to one another. Such a position, not nested in some narrow valley, not pinnacled in the inane, but on the heights, is the best position for a teacher of civil prudence. It is there that those *axiomata media*, of the importance of which Bacon has spoken, are most readily and as it were inevitably apprehended. The politician who is guided from day to day by the maxims of hand-to-mouth expediency seemed to Burke to be unworthy of the name of a politician ; and yet Burke held that expediency in a larger sense is the true rule in politics. "People not very well grounded in the principles of public morality," he says, "find a set of maxims in office ready made for them, which they assume as naturally and inevitably as any of the insignia of the situation. A certain tone of the solid and practical is immediately acquired. Every former profession of public spirit is to be considered as a debauch of youth, or, at best, as a visionary scheme of unattainable perfection. The very idea of consistency is exploded. The convenience of the business of the day is to furnish the principle for doing it." In a well-known passage of the speech on American taxation Burke traces the errors of

Grenville, whose masculine understanding and resolute heart he applauds, first to the narrowing influence of the legal profession, which, though admirable in its power to quicken and invigorate the intellect, is not apt, he says, to open and liberalize the mind in the same proportion ; and, secondly, to the fact that on quitting the profession of the law, Grenville plunged into the business of office and the limited and fixed methods and forms established there. " Persons who are nurtured in office," Burke writes, " do admirably well as long as things go on in their common order ; but when the highroads are broken up, and the waters out, when a new and troubled scene is opened, and the file affords no precedent, then it is that a greater knowledge of mankind and a far more extensive comprehension of things is requisite than ever office gave, or than office can ever give." Such is one error in the training of a statesman, — for the general principles of civil prudence to substitute mere astuteness and manipulative skill in dealing with details. The other error, that of soaring in search of first principles wholly out of view of reality, is more dangerous. To speculate after a fashion *in vacuo* is easy, and in this manner many difficulties can be evaded by the thinker ;

but it is a cheap and cowardly mode of attaining credit for superior wisdom. To manufacture doctrinaire systems that will not work is, after all, a poor trade, which requires only an unskilled and a pretentious mechanician. In one of his happy phrases Burke censures political metaphysics for their "clumsy subtlety;" the toys are ingenious, and yet their ingenuity is that of a bungler. From the experiences of the French Revolution Godwin learnt to estimate the value of a form of government according to the simplicity of its arrangement. Such simplicity was regarded by Burke as sufficient evidence of inadequacy or entire unsoundness in construction: "The nature of man is intricate; the objects of society are of the greatest possible complexity; and therefore no simple disposition or direction of power can be suitable either to man's nature or to the quality of his affairs. When I hear of simplicity of contrivance aimed at and boasted of in any new political constitutions, I am at no loss to decide that the artificers are grossly ignorant of their trade, or totally negligent of their duty. The simple governments are fundamentally defective, to say no worse of them." Burke's standpoint, then, to which the nature of his mind conducted him,

was neither with the misnamed practical politicians, whose principles of expediency are only a
superior kind of cunning, nor with the system-
mongers, who ignore all details and efface all
distinctions in order to attain a crude or spurious
simplicity. He studied human affairs most ob-
servantly, most laboriously; but he studied them
from the heights, and the general principles
which he accepted were principles which he desired to submit to the test of practice.

What has been said will serve to explain the
apparent anomaly that our wisest political thinker
should often appear hostile to political speculation. With all the fervor of his eloquence
he declaims against theorists; yet Burke was
a theorist himself. Coleridge, when criticising
Burke in "The Friend," declares his belief that
an erroneous system is best confuted, not by an
abuse of theory in general, nor by an absurd
opposition of theory to practice, but by a detec-
tion of the errors in the particular theory, "for
the meanest of men has his theory, and to think
at all is to theorize." And Mackintosh, in a
remarkable estimate of Burke, published post-
humously, while commending Burke for his
resistance to those precipitate generalizations,
which are as much the bane of sound political

theory as they are of safe practice, adds that
from a more elevated position Burke might have
discovered that such hasty generalizations were
as unphilosophical as they were impracticable,
and that "the error consisted not in their being
metaphysical, but in their being false." It is,
indeed, the case that the error lies in the false-
ness of such generalizations; but this is precisely
what Burke himself has said. He talks, it is
true, with passionate contempt of "metaphysical
theorists," but his contempt arises not from the
fact that they are theorists; it arises from the
fact that they are, as he puts it in one word,
"sophisters." He could have no claim to the
title of a political thinker if he despised ideas.
Just ideas Burke did not despise. "I do not,"
he says, "put abstract ideas out of the question,
because I well know that under that name I
should dismiss principles, and that without the
guide and light of sound, well-understood principles, all reasonings in politics, as in everything
else, would be only a confused jumble of particular facts and details, without the means of draw-
ing out any theoretical or practical conclusion."
And again: "I do not vilify theory and speculation,—no, because that would be to vilify reason
itself. No: whenever I speak against theory, I

always mean a weak, erroneous, fallacious, un-
founded, or imperfect theory; and one of the
ways of discovering that it is a false theory is
to compare it with practice. This is the true
touchstone of all theories which regard man and
the affairs of men." As a practical statesman,
Burke was naturally led to disprove erroneous
theories by considering them in the light of practice rather than by seeking that more elevated
platform of philosophy recommended by Mackintosh.

Burke then, as he says, did not vilify theory
and speculation. In what respect were the theories against which he declaimed erroneous or
incomplete? This was common to them, — and
it is characteristic of the Revolutionary way of
thought, — they overlooked or omitted an essential part of the facts; they omitted the circumstances of the case, and yet, in a right view,
the circumstances formed an important part of
the case. They reduced things concrete to speculative abstractions. The eighteenth-century
classical spirit in literature, with its generaliz-
ing tendency, and its passion for barren per-
sonification, had united with the methods of
geometrical science, and was now applying itself to political thought. "Man" was spoken

of, and the "Rights of Man;" by "man" was
signified not the actual men to whom presently
the doctrine was applied, not men as formed
by society and surrounded with all its complex
and varying conditions, but some bare metaphysical entity of the philosopher's own invention. Government was the subject of conflicting
theories; not this government or that, with a
history and an environment, to which, however,
the theory was about to be fitted, but some
abstract government as ideal as the geometer's
point or line or circle, — some government denuded of everything substantial, and such as
had never existed on this earth. All such theories, according to Burke, are necessarily false
theories. "Nothing universal," he maintains,
"can be rationally affirmed on any moral or any
political subject. Pure metaphysical abstraction
does not belong to these matters. The lines of
morality are not like ideal lines of mathematics.
They are broad and deep as well as long. They
admit of exceptions; they demand modifications.
These exceptions and modifications are not made
by the process of logic, but by the rules of prudence. Prudence is not only the first in rank of
the virtues political and moral, but she is the
director, the regulator, the standard of them all."

"Circumstances," he writes again, "(which with some gentlemen pass for nothing) give in reality to every political principle its distinguishing color and discriminating effect. The circumstances are what render every civil or political scheme beneficial or noxious to mankind."

Burke, then, our highest teacher of political wisdom, was himself a speculator, a reasoner in politics; but he tried to reason and to speculate with the facts of the case before him. The late Sir J. Fitzjames Stephen, in one of several excellent articles on Burke, printed in the third volume of his "Horæ Sabbaticæ," asserts that Burke was an *à priori* reasoner. It is true that in forming a theory of society, its nature and the duties of its members, he investigates and interprets the facts in the light of his own moral nature. He brings his total self to bear upon the subject of his inquiry. Burke's nature, complete in all the parts and passions of manhood, was profoundly religious. In the irreparable affliction of his old age, the loss of that son around whom all his deep affection, his pride, his fond hopes had gathered, he suffered with such resignation as was possible to the Divine will: "I am stripped of all my honors, I am torn up by the roots and lie prostrate on the earth.

There, and prostrate there, I most unfeignedly recognize the Divine justice, and in some degree submit to it." In the same "Letter to a Noble Lord," in which these sentences occur, there is a yet more comfortable word for those who are called on to toil or to endure in the years of our infirmity: "No man lives too long who lives to do with spirit, or suffer with resignation, what Providence pleases to command or inflict, and indeed they are sharp incommodities which beset old age." Such was the temper of Burke's mind; and when he came to think on social questions, he must needs think in the way which the facts of his own moral nature justified. "Like Berkeley," wrote Sir Fitzjames Stephen, "whose philosophy harmonizes singularly with Burke's writings, and in all probability had powerfully affected his mind, Burke makes duty to God the foundation of everything else; and also, like Berkeley, he referred to the will and disposition of God all the principal relations between man and man, and regarded the great moral duties, and the rights which arise out of them, as divinely instituted, and superior in kind and degree to all other obligations whatever." There is, indeed, something in common between Godwin, whose theory of human society when he

wrote " Political Justice " was atheistic, and
Burke. Justice, according to Godwin, is ante-
cedent to human law; all that law can do is
to interpret the principles of justice; it cannot
create them. The same doctrine is maintained
by Burke, with this difference, that the order
of nature and of society was held by him to
be a divinely instituted order. Mr. John Morley
speaks of a certain mysticism which lay at the
bottom of all Burke's thoughts about communities and governments: " To him there was an
element of mystery in the cohesion of men in
societies, in political obedience, in the sanctity
of contract; in all that fabric of law and charter
and obligation, whether written or unwritten,
which is the sheltering bulwark between civilization and barbarism." When he wrote these
words, Mr. Morley not improbably had in his
memory a passage from Burke in which he con-
templates with wonder and admiration the transitoriness and the continuity of human society.
An order has been appointed by our Divine
Ruler for the successive generations of mankind:
" A mode of existence decreed to a permanent
body composed of transitory parts, wherein,
by the disposition of a stupendous wisdom
moulding together the great mysterious incor-

poration of the human race, the whole at one
time is never old or middle-aged or young;
but in a condition of unchangeable constancy
moves on through the varied tenor of perpetual
decay, full of renovation and progression. . . .
The awful Author of our being is the Author
of our place in the order of existence; and having disposed and marshalled us by a divine tac-
tic, not according to our will, but according to
his, he has in and by that disposition virtually
subjected us to act the part which belongs to the
place assigned us." If to believe that the order
of the world is a Providential order be mysticism,
then the teaching of Burke may be described as
political mysticism. Perhaps, however, it falls
short of that mysticism affected by Mr. Morley
himself, or by his master in philosophy, which
constructs a Deity out of the transitory atoms
of the human race.

"If Burke's generalities," wrote Fitzjames
Stephen, "are reduced to special cases, they
look very much the reverse of imposing. Did
Burke mean to say that God gave two members
to Old Sarum, and, if not, what precisely does he
mean?" Burke did not mean to say that God
gave two members to Old Sarum; he was far
from alleging that everything in the existing

order of society is of divine and immutable appointment.   His meaning was akin to that of Hooker, who looked to God as the fountain of law, while maintaining that certain laws of ecclesiastical polity — the laws of God's Church — are mutable.   His view of things had much in common with that of another remarkable thinker of the eighteenth century, Bishop Butler, who held that it would be indeed mysticism or unmeaning verbiage to ascribe the order of the world to the words or idea " course of nature," but who believed that this becomes intelligible and full of meaning as soon as we acknowledge that the " course of nature " is equivalent to the operations of an Author of nature, and moral governor of the world ; and who, admitting as he did, all the confusion and disorder in the world, yet contended that the principles and beginnings of a moral government are discernible here and now.   Burke did not mean to say that God gave two members to Old Sarum ; but he did mean that in attempting to reform the Parliamentary representative system we should proceed in the spirit which Butler describes as befitting such creatures as men — " a settled moderation and reasonableness of temper, the contrary both to thoughtless levity and also to that unrestrained

self-will . . . which may be observed in undisciplined minds;" and that if we proceed to abolish
the representation of Old Sarum in this spirit, the
spirit of reform and not of revolution, we shall, as
Butler puts it, "be on the side of the Divine administration and co-operating with it." If Burke's
generalities tend to beget this temper, the gain is
not inconsiderable, and it matters little whether,
when reduced to special cases, they look imposing
or the reverse.

With his devout reverence for a Divine order,
not fully realized, yet ever present, in human
society and human institutions, Burke's imagination co-operated. It is common to speak of him
as a great prose poet, and the critics who so describe him commonly cite in illustration some
passage brilliant with the colors of a rhetorician's
art. In general Burke's imagery is not for orna-
ment, but for use; it is, as De Quincey justly
observes, not the mere dressing of his thought,
but the body in which his thought is incarnated
and through which it operates. But if we would
really bring home to ourselves the power of
Burke's imagination, we should think less of this
or that passage of resplendent eloquence than of
his constant imaginative realization of the greatness and the majesty of social order. There is

much that we encounter in life from day to day which tends to kill or to enfeeble our sense of the dignity of human life.   The dross and slag of the world accumulate around us; as we advance in manhood, how high the pile has grown!   The smoke becomes denser as morning deepens to noon; the smuts drop on our hands and faces; life looks, after all, a poor affair.   But the worth, the grace, the majesty of human existence none the less survive; and if only the imagination could be set free, we should feel that such is the fact.   We move about, even in this visible sphere, in worlds not realized.   So it is in our domestic life, in the communities of the hearth and the home.   The cares of each day are too apt to fill our hearts as it were with dust; the petty anxieties, the petty difficulties, the trivial round, the tedium, the monotony of the weeks, dull our sense of what is beautiful.   And then perhaps death comes, and our imaginative power is liberated — too late for its best uses — and we recognize the hidden lines of beauty, and perceive in its fulness the half-apprehended joy.   Happy is he who with the aid of a wisely informed imagination discovers in good time the beauty of his own daily life.   To conceive aright the greatness and majesty of a nation's life demands a larger and

richer imagination. It is cleverer, no doubt, to
be daintily critical, to be elegantly cynical; but
the cleverness is of a somewhat cheap kind.
Edgar Poe speaks of "the glory that was Greece,
and the grandeur that was Rome." Those ancient
civilizations have passed away; we see in imagination their forms, enfranchised from what was
unlovely, as we see the forms of the dead. But
have we no thought to think, no word to say of
the grandeur that is England or of the glory that
is America? Are we even unable "to feel"—in
Wordsworth's memorable phrase—"that we are
greater than we know"? Burke, assuredly, was
not aware that to revere one's country and to
honor her people is an offence against the refinement of culture; when he spoke of the splendid
inheritance which Englishmen have received
from their forefathers, his imagination as a poet
was not inventing imagery or constructing
phrases, but, as he believed, was discovering
truth. If it be not good manners to glory in
ourselves and our own possessions, or, as some
would say, to beat the big drum to the tune of
"Rule Britannia," we may listen for a moment or
two to Burke as he speaks of a country that is not
ours: "When I consider the face of the kingdom
of France; the multitude and opulence of her

cities; the useful magnificence of her spacious highroads and bridges; the opportunity of her artificial canals and navigations, opening the conveniences of maritime communication through a solid continent of so immense an extent; when I turn my eyes to the stupendous works of her ports and harbors, and to her whole naval apparatus whether for war or trade; when I bring before my view the number of her fortifications, constructed with so bold and masterly a skill, and made and maintained at so prodigious a charge, presenting an armed front and impenetrable barrier to her enemies upon every side; when I recollect how very small a part of that extensive region is without cultivation, and to what complete perfection the culture of many of the best productions of the earth have been brought in France; when I reflect on the excellence of her manufactures and fabrics, second to none but ours, and in some particulars not second; when I contemplate the grand foundations of charity, public and private; when I survey the state of all the arts that beautify and polish life; when I reckon the men she has bred for extending her fame in war, her able statesmen, the multitude of her profound lawyers and theologians, her philosophers, her critics, her historians and antiquaries, her poets and her orators, sacred and profane, — I behold in all this something which awes and commands the imagination, which checks the mind on the brink of precipitate and indiscriminating censure, and which demands that we should very seriously examine what and how great are the latent vices that could authorize us at once to level so specious a fabric with the ground." In this stately enumeration there is no imagery; but the imagination orders its materials with an architectonic power and to majestic results. With such an imagination the conservative temper of Burke was closely connected. It is true that in this passage Burke presents only one side of things; another and a different enumeration, an inventory of vices and miseries — latent and patent — had been possible. Burke's point of view presents at least one important aspect of the truth, and an aspect which his opponents were willing to disregard. The cumulative method of the passage produces, without any rhetorical outburst, the effect of the swells of an organ, broadening and prolonging the volume of the central thought; we begin with the highroads and bridges; we close with the historians, the orators, and the poets.

"He saw life steadily," says Matthew Arnold of Sophocles, "and saw it whole." One of Burke's critics, Mr. Augustine Birrell, substituting for the word "life" the words "organized society," adopts the sentence and applies it, so altered, to Burke. "He knew," writes Mr. Birrell,[1] "how the whole world lived. Everything contributed to this; his vast desultory reading, his education, his wanderings up and down the country, his vast conversational powers, his enormous correspondence, his unfailing interest in all pursuits, trades, manufactures, — all helped to keep before him, like motes dancing in a sunbeam, the huge organism of modern society. Burke's imagination led him to look out over the whole land; the legislator devising new laws, the judge expounding and enforcing old ones, the merchant despatching his goods and extending his credit, the ancient institutions of Church and University with their seemly provisions for sound learning and true religion, the parson in his pulpit, the poet pondering his rhymes, the farmer eying his crops, the painter covering his canvases, the player educating the feelings, — Burke saw all this with the fancy of a poet, and dwelt on it with the eye

[1] The passage from "Obiter Dicta" (second series) is here abbreviated.

of a lover. But love is the parent of fear, and none knew better than Burke how thin is the lava layer between the costly fabric of society and the volcanic heats and destroying flames of anarchy." It was impossible that the conclusions of a thinker who saw men thus could be identical with the conclusions of one who saw men as mathematical units, each like every other, stripped of all distinctions, and each equal to every other.

To see the life of society in this rich, concrete, imaginative way, was to supply political passion with its appropriate nutriment. When Godwin speculated, he endeavored to make his whole mind a mere organ of the reason. His aim and his pride were to argue with the coldness and the precision of a machine. Yet there were wild-eyed hopes which peered through the grates of Godwin's argument; and if he did not exercise his imagination in vivifying and interpreting the facts of existing society, his imagination had its revenge. Cut off from the sustenance and support of reality, it created that dream of the future life of man on earth, which Shelley afterwards glorified with the iridescent colors of his poetry. The passions of the Revolution lived in Godwin, and roused his intellect in the search for first principles ; but he failed to recognize them as among the sources of his own tendency to generalization, and he attempted to cut his understanding off from its vivifying springs in the heart. Burke never doubted that passion aids a thinker in the discovery of truth. "Political truth," Mackintosh writes in his criticism of Burke, " seems, as it were, to lie too deep to be reached by calm labor, and it appears to be only thrown up from the recesses of a great understanding by the powerful agency of those passions which the contests of politics inspire." Burke's heart was as large and fervid as his intellect. His domestic affections were deep-seated and constant. How he was shaken and broken by the death of his son has been described by his friend O'Beirne, Bishop of Meath. In the records of sorrow there are few incidents more affecting — and it is none the less affecting because it touches the ludicrous — than that which tells of the sudden wave of grief which overwhelmed the aged man when at Beaconsfield the worn-out horse, formerly ridden by his son, approached him and rested its head against his breast ; in an instant Burke's firmness gave way to an agony of recollection, and, throwing his arms over his old follower's neck, he wept loudly and long.

It would be untrue to say that in his political writings Burke's passions did not at times obscure or overmaster his judgment; they aggrandize one mass of facts until another is hidden from view; they render him an impatient listener to his adversary's case. But far more frequently Burke's reason was stimulated and illuminated by his feelings. When he showed Francis some proof-sheets of the "Reflections on the French Revolution," his critic assured him that the well-known passage about Marie Antoinette was "pure foppery." "I tell you again," Burke replied, "that the recollection of the manner in which I saw the Queen of France in the year 1774, and the contrast between that brilliancy, splendor, and beauty, with the prostrate homage of a nation to her, and the abominable scene of 1789, which I was describing, *did* draw tears from me and wetted my paper. These tears came again into my eyes as often as I looked at the description, — they may again." The feeling was natural to Burke, and, as he says, "in those natural feelings we learn great lessons." "Men are we," exclaims Wordsworth, in his sonnet on the extinction of the Venetian Republic, —

"Men are we, and must grieve when even the shade
Of that which once was great is passed away."

There is no true wisdom in seeking to transcend the elementary passions of our humanity. "Why," Burke asks, "do I feel so differently from the Rev. Dr. Price, and those of his lay flock, who will choose to adopt the sentiments of his discourse? For this plain reason, — because it is natural I should; because we are so made as to be affected at such spectacles with melancholy sentiments upon the unstable condition of mortal prosperity, and the tremendous uncertainty of human greatness; . . . because in events like these our passions instruct our reason; . . . we are alarmed into reflection; our minds (as it has long since been observed) are purified by terror and pity; our weak, unthinking pride is humbled under the dispensations of a mysterious wisdom." And again, in defence of emotion as an adjunct and an aid to reason: "Never was there a jar or discord between genuine sentiment and sound policy. Never, no, never, did Nature say one thing and Wisdom say another. Nor are sentiments of elevation in themselves turgid and unnatural. . . . It is when a great nation is in great difficulties that minds must exalt themselves to the occasion, or all is lost. Strong passions, under the direction of a feeble reason, feed a low fever, which serves only to destroy the body that entertains it. But vehement passion does not always indicate an infirm judgment. It often accompanies, and actuates, and is even auxiliary to a powerful understanding : and when they both conspire and act harmoniously, their force is great to destroy disorder within and to repel injury from abroad."

Burke's outbreaks of passionate pity for the royal family, for the aristocracy and the clergy, of France were met in his own day with the cry of sentimentalism. Had he no sympathy with the victims of monarchy, — with the peasant ground down by taxes, with the serfs of the Church, with those who languished in the prisons of France ? In a phrase which was remembered and afterwards served Shelley as the motto for a pamphlet, Paine retorted upon Burke : " He pities the plumage, and forgets the dying bird. . . . His hero or his heroine must be a tragedy-victim expiring in show, and not the real prisoner of misery, sliding into death in the silence of a dungeon." Mary Wollstonecraft adopted the same line of comment. " It was," writes that able and sympathetic critic, Mr. Morley, " no idle abstraction, no metaphysical right of man, for which the French cried, but only the practical right of being permitted by their own toil to save themselves and the little ones about their knees from hunger and cruel death." It was for both material relief and for metaphysical rights that the cry went up ; and the material claims were based by the exponents of the Revolution on the metaphysical rights. We should at least bear in mind the fact that Burke's feelings towards those sufferers with whose griefs he came directly into contact, were not merely rhetorical, and were proved to be genuine by self-sacrifice. Leaders of the Revolution declaimed in Paris concerning liberty and fraternity, while their hands were red with blood from the prison massacres. Burke did more than declaim ; he founded a school for the destitute children of those who had perished by the guillotine or the assassin's knife, and until the close of his life he watched over it with the tenderest solicitude. As to the social condition of France prior to the Revolution, Burke, as Mr. Morley tells us, was imperfectly informed. Arthur Young's "Travels in France" was not published until after the "Reflections" had appeared. But had his information been far less incomplete, we may be assured that Burke would have remained of the opinion that there were other and better ways of amending the condition of the French peasant and artisan than the way of over-

throwing existing institutions, — the way of confiscation, of massacre, and the theatrical worship
of Reason. Burke's whole mind and strength
and life had been devoted to the service of his
fellows, — not of a class, not of an aristocracy, but
of the people. He had been the advocate of freedom of trade (I cite a portion of Buckle's enumeration of the great measures of later times which
Burke anticipated and supported); he pleaded
for the just claims of the Catholics, which during
his lifetime were refused; he urged that dissenters should be relieved from oppressive ecclesiastical restrictions; he opposed the cruel laws
against insolvents; he vainly attempted to soften
the Penal Code; he desired to abolish the hard-
ship of enlisting soldiers for life; he attacked the
slave-trade, which the king wished to preserve as
part of the British constitution; he was one of
the first and one of the ablest financial reformers
in Parliament.[1] The benefits which Burke endeavored to obtain were benefits for the people;
if they have been won by others than him, they
were won in Burke's way of reform, not by the
sanguinary process of a revolution leading directly
to an enormous military tyranny.   Did Burke

[1] Buckle, History of Civilization in England, vol. i. pp. 462–
464.

then pity the plumage and forget the dying bird?
The answer is that, right or wrong, he did not
believe that plucking away the plumage was the
best way of restoring the dying bird to vigor and
enabling it to fly.

Burke, then, was not of opinion that the cause
of suffering humanity could be really served by a
system of ideas which he held to be false, by
methods which he considered criminal, and by
men who seemed to him to be at best pretentious
bunglers. "To innovate," he says, "is not to reform. The French revolutionists complained of
everything; they refused to reform anything; and
they left nothing, no, nothing at all, unchanged.
The consequences are *before* us, — not in remote
history, not in future prognostication; they are
about us, they are upon us. They shake the
public security; they menace private enjoyment.
They dwarf the growth of the young; they break
the quiet of the old." Burke would at once conserve and reform; the obstinacy which rejects
all improvement, and the levity that is fatigued
with everything actual, seemed to him to be alike
vices. But such a process of reform, it is ob-
jected, is slow; it might take up many years.
"Without question," Burke replies, "it might;
and it ought." Each year, however, would give

proof of the soundness of the method. The Revolution, which changed everything of a sudden,
had certainly not brought immediate happiness to
France. Its defenders, as at all times the defenders of violent and criminal methods are compelled to do, prophesied a glorious future. " It is
remarkable," wrote Burke, " that they never see
their way to their projected good but by the road
to some evil. . . . Their humanity is at their
horizon, and, like the horizon, it always flies before them." Meanwhile men and women might
suffer ; if only the cause progressed, if only the
idea was maintained, all must be well: " These
philosophers consider men in their experiments
no more than they do mice in an air-pump, or in
a recipient of mephitic gas." The burden of
proof lay heavily, as Burke held, on those who
tore to pieces the whole frame and contexture of
their country, that no other method of attaining
wise government than the way of violence, which
caused such widespread immediate misery, would
have succeeded. " Men have no right," he said,
" to put the well-being of the present generation
wholly out of the question. Perhaps the only
moral trust with any certainty in our hands is
the care of our own time. With regard to futu-
rity, we are to treat it like a ward. We are not

so to attempt an improvement of his fortune as to put the capital of his estate to any hazard."

Burke, as Mr. Morley states, had insufficient acquaintance with the social condition of France. But he was no idealist enamoured of the feudal régime. He admitted that the French government before the Revolution, though the best of "the unqualified or ill-qualified monarchies," was full of abuses. "Upon a free Constitution," he wrote, "there was but one opinion in France. The absolute monarchy was at an end. It breathed its last without a groan, without a struggle, without convulsion. All the struggle arose afterwards, upon the preference of a despotic democracy to a government of reciprocal control." When he advocated war against the Republic, he did so with no view of restoring a despotic monarchy as a substitute for anarchy. To a Republic, considered in the abstract, he could not be opposed. The Republic of Berne he speaks of as one of the most happy, the most prosperous, and the best governed countries upon earth ; and he lamented that it was one of the great objects at the destruction of which the French Revolutionary party aimed. Neither monarchy in the abstract nor a democracy in the abstract could receive praise or condemnation from him ;

he would consider nothing without its circumstances. Speaking in an abstract way, liberty and government are both needful. "Old as I am," he wrote, "I read the fine raptures of Lucan and Corneille with pleasure;" but the moment we come to deal with human affairs we must put the questions — What kind of liberty? What kind of government? The liberty of a madman escaped from the asylum is not a thing to elate our hearts; we do not congratulate a highwayman who has broken from jail on the recovery of his natural rights. What Burke cherished is "a manly, moral, regulated liberty," coincident with order. "Men," he says, "must have a certain fund of natural moderation to qualify them for freedom, else it becomes noxious to themselves and a perfect nuisance to everybody else." Looking at the facts before him, he could not see that France had attained, or was on the way to attain, a rational freedom. "When I shall learn that in France the citizen, by whatever description he is qualified, is in a perfect state of legal security with regard to his life, to his property, to the uncontrolled disposal of his person, to the free use of his industry and his faculties . . . when I am assured that a simple citizen may decently express his sentiments upon

public affairs without hazard to his life or liberty, even against a predominant and fashionable
opinion, — when I know all this of France, I shall
be as well pleased as any one must be who has
not forgot the general communion of mankind
. . . in local and accidental sympathies." Burke
does not deny what he calls the real rights of
men ; but these are rights of society, not of un-
covenanted nature ; and among such rights not
the least important are certain restraints. In
the partnership of human beings which constitutes society, all men have their rights ; all men
have equal rights, but not to equal things. The
right of each man to this or to that is settled
by convention ; not by nature, but by a kind of
social fine art, which is indeed nature at one
remove, for art, as Burke puts it, is man's
nature.

Burke, undoubtedly, saw only a portion of the
great phenomenon which was unrolling itself
before Europe. He laid himself open to rebuke
by an imperfection of vision, by excesses of
temper, and by undiscriminating extravagances
of statement. "Mackintosh," writes Mr. Morley, "replied to the 'Reflections' with manli-
ness and temperance in the 'Vindiciæ Gallicæ.'
Thomas Paine replied to them with an energy,

courage, and eloquence worthy of his cause in the 'Rights of Man.' But the substantial and decisive reply to Burke came from his former correspondent, the farmer at Bradfield in Suffolk. Arthur Young published his 'Travels in France' some eighteen months after the 'Reflections' (1792); and the pages of the twenty-first chapter, in which he closes his performance, as a luminous criticism of the most important side of the Revolution, are worth a hundred times more than Burke, Mackintosh, and Paine all put together. Young afterwards became panic-stricken, but his book remained. There the writer plainly enumerates without trope or invective the intolerable burdens under which the great mass of the French people had for years been groaning." But Burke's contention was not in favor of the old régime ; though his sense of the oppression of the French peasantry was inadequate, he admitted the abuses of the government. His contention was that the Revolutionary method of remedying abuses was an unsound method, and that it had not led to happy results. Young's " Travels in France," far from constituting a " substantial and decisive reply " to Burke, supports his conclusions. A change in France, a reform or a series of

reforms, had, in Young's opinion, become a
necessity; but he held with Burke that a constitutional reform was possible, and that unmeas-
ured evils had been brought upon the country
by the Revolution. It was not only the nobility or the clergy who were the sufferers; manufactures decayed; many thousands of families
were condemned to death by starvation. Young
had himself seen the miserable wretches at
Lyons, at Abbeville, at Amiens. He had a
faith that the effects of the Revolution on the
small landed proprietors must "in the end" be
happy; but under the system adopted by the
Assembly he declares, with the emphasis of
capital letters, "Agriculture cannot flourish."
He maintains that to effect all that was necessary, it did not require that "all France should
be overthrown, ranks annihilated, property attacked, the monarchy abolished," civil war rendered imminent. No; he was of Burke's opinion.
"France," he writes, "might have been free without violence. . . . The weight of the commons
would have been predominant; but it would
have had checks and a control, without which
power is not constitution, but *tyranny*." As he
wrote thus, Young regarded the Revolution with
more favor than he did a year later, when he

could study its fuller development. In 1793 he wrote still cautiously, not in a panic but with fresh facts before him. He tells the reader of his pamphlet " The Example of France a Warning to Britain," that he has a constitutional abhorrence of theory; he is a farmer, who patiently observes positive facts; he will speak only of the results of the great political experiment. He considers, first, the actual state of France, and, secondly, the causes of her ills, before applying her warning example to the landed, moneyed, commercial, and laboring interests of Great Britain. " We may say with truth and moderation," writes Young, " that [the new French constitution] has brought more misery, poverty, devastation, imprisonment, bloodshed, and ruin on France in four years than the old government did in a century." The state of France as regards the personal liberty of her subjects he describes in five words, — *there is no such thing*. " A gigantic and devouring despotism has levelled in the dust all security to those whose properties raise them above the mob." Young, Mr. Morley tells us, knew of the intolerable burdens under which the French people had groaned. What is his statement ? (and he wrote, not as a Tory, but as a friend to reform in England.) " The old govern-

ment of France," he declares, " with all its faults,
was certainly the best enjoyed by any considerable country in Europe, England alone excepted;
but there were many faults in it which every
class of the people wished to remedy. . . . At
the commencement of the Revolution, France
possessed a very flourishing commerce, the rich-
est colonies in the world, the greatest currency
of solid money in Europe; her agriculture was
improving; and her people, though from too
great a population, much too numerous for the
highest degrees of national prosperity, were yet
more at their ease than in many other countries
of Europe; the government was regular and mild.
. . . Her present state may thus with truth be
described: Her government an anarchy that
values neither life nor property; her agriculture
fast sinking, her farmers the slaves of all, and
her people starving; her manufactures annihilated, her commerce destroyed, and her colonies
absolutely ruined; her gold and silver disappeared; her national revenue diminished three-
fourths; her cities scenes of revolt, of massacre
and starvation; and her provinces plundered by
gangs of banditti. . . . It is the legislation of
wolves that govern only by destruction; and all
these massacres, and plunderings, and burnings,

and horrors of every denomination are so far from being necessary for the establishment of liberty that they have most effectually destroyed it."

So much for the testimony of Arthur Young, both in his Travels and his pamphlet. Paine, Mr. Morley informs us, replied to Burke's " Reflections " "in a manner worthy of his cause." Apparently the Cause was not worthy of Thomas Paine. In 1793 he was elected to the Convention as deputy for the Pas de Calais; a little later he was arrested, imprisoned, and denounced. " The state of things in the prisons," he says, " was a continued scene of horror. No man could count upon life for twenty-four hours." What he desired above all else was "forgetfulness." Thanks to the efforts of his adopted countrymen, he was liberated as an American citizen. While remaining faithful to his Republican principles, he has to describe the Revolutionary government as " a thing without either principle or authority." "Virtue or crime," he says, " depended on accident, and that which was patriotism one day became treason the next." As to Mackintosh, whose " Vindiciæ Gallicæ" Mr. Morley justly commends, it should not be forgotten that he made a manly recantation of his earlier opinions, and sought for the friendship of Burke. "From the earliest moment of reflection," he wrote, "your writings were my chief study and delight. . . . For a time, indeed, seduced by the love of what I thought liberty, I ventured to oppose, without ever ceasing to venerate, that writer who had nourished my understanding with the most wholesome principles of political wisdom. I speak to state facts, not to flatter: you are above flattery, and, permit me to say, I am too proud to flatter even you." Mr. Morley can hardly be accounted happy in his choice of witnesses against Burke.

Trained to public life as a member of the Whig party of the eighteenth century, Burke in his sympathies was aristocratical. He speaks of the People as a venerable object; but it was a disciplined, ordered people that he regarded with veneration; in the people reduced to a mob of jarring atoms he saw only a disbanded race of deserters and vagabonds. "For a while they may be terrible indeed; but in such manner as wild beasts are terrible. The mind owes to them no sort of submission." Here is the explanation of the words which roused such strong indignation among Burke's opponents, and which were so often turned against him, — "the swinish multitude." The multitude, according to Burke, is not swinish while it forms a true People; then it is venerable and mysteriously sacred: but a disorganized mob is not the People; it is a "disbanded race of deserters;" it may soon acquire the rapacity, the ferocity, the dulness, the grossness of the beast. For the sake not of a class but of the whole people he estimated highly the value of what he terms a natural aristocracy; he views such an aristocracy not as a separate interest in the state nor as separable from it. Its origin is in nature, and in the facts of social life which are a part of nature: "To be bred in a place of estimation; to see nothing low or sordid from one's infancy; to be taught to respect oneself; to be habituated to the censorial inspection of the public eye; to look early to public opinion; to stand upon such elevated ground as to be enabled to take a large view of the widespread and infinitely diversified combinations of men and affairs in a large society; to have leisure to read, to reflect, to converse; to be enabled to draw the court and attention of the wise and learned wherever they are to be found; to be habituated in armies to command and to obey; to be taught to despise dangers in the pursuit of honor and duty; to be formed to the greatest degree of vigilance, foresight, and circumspection, in a state of things in

which no fault is committed with impunity, and
the slightest mistakes draw on the most ruinous
consequences; to be led to a guarded and regulated conduct, from a sense that you are considered an instructor of your fellow-citizens in their
highest concerns, and that you act as a reconciler
between God and man; to be employed as an ad-
ministrator of law and justice, and to be thereby
amongst the first benefactors of mankind; to be
a professor of high science or of liberal and in-
genuous art; to be amongst rich traders who
from their success are presumed to have sharp
and vigorous understandings, and to possess the
virtues of diligence, order, constancy, and regu-
larity, and to have cultivated an habitual regard
to commutative justice, — these are the circumstances of men which form what I should call a
natural aristocracy, without which there is no
nation."

Even the prejudices created by rank and station were not viewed with entire disfavor by
Burke. "That a man should be looked up to
with servility and awe," wrote Godwin in "Political Justice," "because the king has bestowed
on him a spurious name, or decorated him with a
ribband; that another should wallow in luxury,
because his ancestor three centuries ago bled in the

quarrel of Lancaster and York, — do we imagine that these iniquities can be practised without injury?" Such a violent outcry against aristocracy Burke took to be a mere work of art. "To be honored," he says, "and even privileged by the laws, opinions, and inveterate usages of our country, growing out of the prejudice of ages, has nothing to provoke horror or indignation in any man." For even in prejudices there lay, as Burke conceived, a certain sanctity and a certain utility. He boldly asserts that he will cherish old prejudices for the reason that they are old. The long life of a prejudice argues in favor of its containing some latent wisdom : " We are afraid to put men to live and trade each on his own private stock of reason, because we suspect that the stock in each man is small, and that the individuals would do better to avail themselves of the general bank and capital of nations and of ages. Many of our men of speculation instead of exploding general prejudices employ their sagacity to discover the latent wisdom which prevails in them." Even from superstition resources may be derived for the public advantage — that is to say, not from the untruths of superstition, but from its hidden truth. The movement of thought in the nineteenth century has been along the line indicated by Burke; the Revolutionary rage against the past beliefs of mankind has given place to an historical study of their origins and their significance. When Mill pointed to Coleridge as dividing with Bentham the best mind of the age, — Bentham asking in regard to any ancient or received opinion the question, Is it true? and Coleridge asking, What is the meaning of it? — he might have added that Coleridge in his way of thinking was in fact the follower of Burke.

Burke's view of the Revolution was incomplete; he was not fully informed, and perhaps he did not sufficiently allow for the recuperative forces of society working in and through and after a great cataclysm. But he expressed, with incomparable power, one entire side of the truth. And his wisdom was confirmed by events. "Oh, heavenly philanthropists," exclaimed Price, in a speech on the occasion of the first anniversary of the fall of the Bastille, "well do you deserve the admiration not only of your own country, but of all countries! You have already determined to renounce forever all wars of conquest and all offensive wars. This is an instance of wisdom and attention to human rights which has no example. But you will do more; you will invite Great Britain to join you in this determination, and to enter into a compact with you for promoting peace on earth, good will among men. . . . Thus united, the two kingdoms will be omnipotent." [1] Such was the political prediction in July, 1790, of a Revolutionary optimist. In November of the same year — still in the golden days of the Revolution — appeared Burke's "Reflections." Mr. Lecky has gathered together some of its anticipations of things to come. Burke predicted the transitoriness of the new government, the fall in the value of paper money, the confiscation of Church property, the national bankruptcy, the destruction of the monarchy, the abolition of the Christian religion, the transference of power to the hands of the most extreme and violent party. He added that the anarchy of the Revolution would close with a military despotism. "The officers of the army," he said, "will remain for some time mutinous and full of faction, until some popular general who understands the art of conciliating the soldiery and who possesses the true spirit of command shall draw the eyes of all men upon himself. Armies will obey him on his personal account. . . . But the moment in which that event

[1] Quoted by Lecky, England in the Eighteenth Century, vol. v. pp. 450, 451.

shall happen, the person who really commands
the army is your master; the master (that
is little) of your King, the master of your
Assembly, the master of your whole republic."
Burke's prophecies were fulfilled to the letter.
His vision did not advance to the remote future.
He did not describe the recuperative energies of
France.   But neither did he describe how France
staggered from Revolution to Revolution, from
monarchy to republic, from republic to empire,
from an empire to a commune, and again to a
republic.   The great movement inaugurated in
1789 has not yet reached its term; we have seen
a century of its evolution with mingled good and
evil.   It was much that Burke, as early as 1790,
discerned the portentous figure of Napoleon
Bonaparte.[1]

[1] Since this lecture was delivered, Princeton University has
made two valuable additions to the study of Burke, — Professor
Woodrow Wilson's essay, " An Interpreter of English Liberty,"
in his volume " Mere Literature ; " and Professor Perry's " Selections from Edmund Burke," with an Introduction, notes, and
bibliography.

IV

EARLY REVOLUTIONARY GROUP AND
ANTAGONISTS: SOUTHEY, COLERIDGE,
THE "ANTI-JACOBIN" (WITH A NOTE
ON BURNS).

EARLY REVOLUTIONARY GROUP AND ANTAGONISTS

WHEN the Revolutionary uprising in France concentrated upon itself the attention of Europe, the original work of Cowper as a poet was virtually ended. From 1785 until 1791 he was chiefly occupied with his translation of Homer. After that date he employed himself upon a translation of Milton's Latin poems. The verses "To Mary" and his last original verses, "The Castaway," show that amid sadness and gloom the poet still lived within him. He was, however, far removed from the possibility of seizing and interpreting the public passions of the time. Another poet, who died four years before Cowper, is at once a predecessor and a contemporary of the Revolution. The Kilmarnock edition of the poems of Burns appeared in 1786 ; his death took place ten years later, in the summer of 1796. While preeminently a national poet, he was more than national; he belonged in a true sense to the European movement of his time. His strength was partly an inheritance from the singers of his native land. It is often said that Burns created Scottish song; it would be more true, observes Principal Shairp, to say that Scottish song created Burns. Not indeed the old ballad poetry of Scotland: if Burns admired such poetry, it did not profoundly influence his art; his imagination was less romantic than passionate. The popular songs, often wedded to melodies gay or pathetic and penetrating, sank into his spirit and became a part of his inmost self. The forms of verse which seem most characteristically his own were caught from his predecessors; the intensity of feeling, the heart of his poetry, was given by his own tender and impetuous heart. Matthew Arnold deplored the fact that the poetry of Burns deals with the unlovely world of Scotch drink, Scotch religion, and Scotch manners. Perhaps it is wise, even in the interests of the highest literature, to be less fastidious; perhaps much genial life, much beauty underlay what seemed unlovely to one whose work is so little rooted in the homely soil, and so largely the outcome of a period of spiritual trouble resulting from the conflict of creeds and cultures. The environment of Burns was not unfavorable

to his genius. He drew strength from the soil.
We cannot wish that he had sung out of the air.
If he was to be inspired by any drink, the most
suitable for Bacchanal enthusiasm was not hydro-
mel or nectar, but the juice " Scotch bear can
mak' us," —

> " Whether thro' wimplin' worms it jink,
>   Or, richly brown, ream owre the brink
>   In glorious faem."

In Scotch manners there was much dignity,
grace, and warm humanity ; and Scotch piety does
not show itself as altogether uncomely in " The
Cotter's Saturday Night."

But the poetry of Burns is more than Scottish ;
it belongs to Europe ; it embodied in local forms
much of the prevailing sentiment of the age.
" The influences under which Burns was tutored
into song," writes one of his critics, " were as eminently European in fact as they were singularly
provincial in appearance. . . . The intellectual
activity and turmoil which led to the Revolution
was a phenomenon to which he was no more of
a stranger in his humble and straitened sphere
of life than to summer's heat or winter's cold.
. . . Burns's poems and songs are a programme
of social and political reform and progress, or at
any rate aspiration, — as radical a programme as

could well be framed. . . . As far as there is any need to characterize his poetical lineage and development, this identifies Burns with the Revolution."[1] In Burns, then, beside the common human element, realized with the utmost intensity, which gives vitality to his best work, there are present at once the Scottish and the wider European influences conjoined, and each playing into the other. He is the pupil of Allan Ramsay, but how different is the tone of the younger poet! What fire, what indignation, what a spirit of revolt have entered into his verse! The contrast is happily pointed by Professor Nichol when he places side by side the "Gentle Shepherd" and the "Jolly Beggars": "The one is a court pastoral, like a minuet of the ladies of Versailles on the sward of the Swiss village near the Trianon ; the other is like the march of the Mænads with Théroigne de Mericourt. . . . The graceless crew are raised above the level of gypsies, footpads, and rogues, and made, like Titans, to launch their thunders of rebellion against the world."

The influence of the French Revolution was to some extent a disturbing influence on the outward life of Burns. An exciseman in the em-

[1] Dr. Service in Ward's The English Poets, vol. iii.

ployment of the government had given pledges to
law and order.   When, in 1792, he purchased the
guns of a condemned smuggler, which had gone
ashore on the sands of the Solway Firth, it was as
a gift for the French legislative body, to which at
the same time he addressed a letter expressing his
admiration and esteem.   Attention was directed
to his conduct, and, full of alarm for his wife and
weans, he wrote to Graham of Fintry a letter in
which he professes the most devoted attachment
to the British Constitution.   At a dinner, when
Pitt's health was proposed, Burns rose and asked
leave to drink to a greater and a better man, —
General Washington.   On another occasion the
toast was even more significant, — "The last
verse of the last chapter of the last Book of
Kings."   Once, according to the report of Charles
Kirkpatrick Sharpe, when at a dramatic performance at Dumfries "God Save the King" was
called for, and the audience stood up uncov-
ered, Burns sat still in the pit with his hat on
his head.   And again he sought the protection of
Graham, with superabundant declarations of loyalty.   "As to France," he says, "I was her enthusiastic votary at the beginning of the business.
When she came to show her old avidity for conquest in annexing Savoy, etc., to her dominions,

and invading the rights of Holland, I altered my sentiments."

By virtue of his ardent and undisciplined temperament, by his peasant origin and his experience of the sufferings of the poor, by that pride of manhood and of genius which made him feel himself an equal of prince or peer, by the zeal of his humanitarian sympathies, by his sentimental Jacobitism and his imaginative enthusiasm for the traditions of Scottish independence, by the fact that he belonged to the democratic Presbyterian Church and sympathized with the party of spiritual revolt, Burns was fitted to be a spokesman of the passions of the time. The passions of the time, for doctrine and theory took little hold on the mind of Burns until they were caught into the kindling heat of passion. M. Angellier, to whose admirable volumes on Burns I gratefully acknowledge my debt, has remarked that so long as the Revolution retained a philosophic and doctrinaire aspect it left Burns almost untouched. "It is only," he writes, "when the Revolution became violent, tragic, and essentially a movement of popular masses, . . . when it ceased to be a declaration of abstract principles, and passed into a conflict of passions," that Burns was deeply moved. Other writers of the time were philosophers or visionaries, who contemplated human affairs from their mounts of speculation.   Burns has rather the aspect of a revolutionary on the barricade, — "The general idea disappears; the passion of the moment breaks forth with something of the rage and fury of the street."[1]   The poet's Revolutionary ardor vented itself chiefly in hasty escapades of action and eager snatches of song; for his nature was essentially lyrical.   When he sang, as a patriotic North Briton, his chant "Does haughty Gaul invasion threat," and declared his adhesion to the party of order, he had still a word to say on behalf of popular rights, —

> "Who will not sing 'God save the King'
>   Shall hang as high 's the steeple;
> But while we sing 'God save the King,'
>   We 'll ne'er forget the People."

It is especially as the poet of Equality — a point justly insisted on by his learned French critic — that Burns belongs to the Revolution. "The rank is but the guinea's stamp," — such is his teaching, — "a man 's a man for a' that."   He had seen and felt early in life the hardships of

---

[1] Robert Burns, tome ii. p. 202.   Burns's authorship of "The Tree of Liberty" (Chambers, vol. iii. pp. 97–99) is, however, discredited.

the toilers in the field.   He had suffered in health
through the severity of labor imposed on him in
boyhood.   He had witnessed the brave struggle
maintained by his father at Mount Oliphant, and
had sung his song of the " Ruined Farmer," —

> " The prosperous man is asleep,
>   Nor hears how the whirlwinds sweep;
>   But Misery and I must watch
>   The surly tempest blow."

At times he expresses his sense of the worth
of manhood with dignity ; at times there breaks
from him a cry of bitter revolt.   He writes to
Mrs. Dunlop in 1789 : " When I must skulk into a
corner, lest the rattling equipage of some gaping
blockhead should mangle me in the mire, I am
tempted to exclaim, ' What merits has he had, or
what demerits have I had, in some state of pre-
existence, that he is ushered into this state of
being with the sceptre of rule and the key of
riches in his puny fist, and I am kicked into the
world the sport of folly, or the victim of pride ? ' "
The Auld Brig of Ayr cannot restrain its indignation against " corky-headed, graceless gentry," —

> " The herryment and ruin of the country ;
>   Men, three-parts made by Tailors and by Barbers."

" A lord," Burns cries in one of the Heron Ballads, may be " a gouk " and creepingly unclean,

"wi' ribbon, star, and a' that." The Newfoundland Cæsar describes to the plebeian collie the manner of life too common among those of high degree; the innocent Luath had supposed that gentlefolk went a-parliamenting in their country's service : —

> "Haith, lad, ye little ken about it;
> For Britain's guid! guid faith! I doubt it.
> Say rather, gaun as Premiers lead him,
> An' saying *aye* or *no* 's they bid him :
> At operas and plays parading,
> Mortgaging, gambling, masquerading."

Abroad at Vienna or Versailles the youth of fashion squanders his paternal estate, or he thrums guitars at Madrid, or swallows German waters to make himself look fair and fat : —

> "There's some exceptions, man and woman,
> But this is gentry's life in common."

"Man," Burns wrote to Mrs. Dunlop, "is by no means a happy creature. I do not speak of the selected few, favored by partial Heaven, whose souls are tuned to gladness amid riches, and honors, and prudence, and wisdom. I speak of the neglected many, whose nerves, whose sinews, whose days, are sold to the minions of fortune." And in a like spirit were composed the tragic stanzas, "Man was made to mourn" : —

> "See yonder poor o'erlabor'd wight,
>   So abject, mean, and vile,
> Who begs a brother of the earth
>   To give him leave to toil;
> And see his lordly fellow-worm
>   The poor petition spurn,
> Unmindful, tho' a weeping wife
>   And helpless offspring mourn."

In such poetry the note is sounded, as M. Angellier expresses it, for the revolt of the proletariat. It is a just observation of the critic that the Revolution in France assisted Burns in purifying his private passion from what was merely egoistic, and in raising his innate feeling in favor of equality to the dignity of a general principle.

So Burns expresses the aggressive or destructive side of the doctrine of human Equality; but as often he expresses the positive side, — a leveller still, but levelling up, by exhibiting the worth of humble life. And at such times he recognizes that there is not only much worth but also much happiness in the cottage. Honest Luath, the collie, has a word to say of the compensations that are found in a poor estate, — repose after fatigue, — "a blink o' rest 's a sweet enjoyment," — the domestic joy of wife and children, —

> "The prattling things are just their pride,
> That sweetens a' their fireside," —

and social mirth and wit, heightened by " twal-
pennie-worth o' nappie." In the admirable
" Epistle to Davie " the same happier spirit is the
prevailing one. Burns confesses that

> "It 's hardly in a body's pow'r
>   To keep, at times, frae being sour,
>   To see how things are shar'd ; "

but he will not dwell on this : he will rather keep
in view the delights and solaces of humble life,
— sunlight of the conscience, wisdom of the heart,
the loyalty of a comrade, the blessedness of love.
The honest man, he elsewhere sings, though of
the poorest, may be a king of men : —

> " What tho' on hamely fare we dine,
>   Wear hodden-gray, and a' that ;
>   Gie fools their silks, and knaves their wine,
>   A man 's a man for a' that."

" I recollect once Burns told me," wrote Dugald
Stewart, " when I was admiring a distant prospect
in one of our morning walks, that the sight of
so many smoking cottages gave a pleasure to his
mind which none could understand who had
not witnessed, like himself, the happiness and
the worth which they contained." Burns has
himself shown us the real nobility and beauty
of a rustic interior in his " Cotter's Saturday
Night." " Never," writes his French biographer

and critic, "has such dignity been shed over the life of the poor. It is a consecration of natural piety, of domestic love, of resignation, of manly honesty, — all found under a lowly roof; a solemn homage to modest virtues." And the ideal presented in the poem is not removed from reality; it is no false Arcadian pastoral, but a fragment of genuine Scottish life and manners. Only, as we read it, we should bear in mind that the democratic sympathies of Burns did not exclude another and a different side of humanity. Over against a "Cotter's Saturday Night," if we would comprehend the genius of its author, we should set his picture of the ragged vagrants' revel by the fireside in Poosie-Nansie's. It is like a picture of Teniers, wrought to higher verve and more abundant animal exaltation than could animate the veins or inspire the imagination of the Flemish artist.

While Burns, the peasant-poet of Equality, was interpreting the new passions of the age, in alternating moods of indignation, love, and pity, the same European influences which affected his art were at play among young and aspiring spirits who were now about to pass from the learned culture of the English universities to creative work in the world of thought and imagination.

Of the three future friends, Wordsworth, Coleridge, and Southey, although Wordsworth felt the concussion of the French Revolution more profoundly, if not earlier, than either of the others, it will be convenient to speak first of Southey and Coleridge, who were brought into close relations, personal and literary, to each other before Wordsworth became a member of the group.

Viewed broadly, the result of the great upheaval in France upon young men of genius who lay open to its influence may be said to have been of a twofold kind : first, emotional, and, secondly, intellectual. It infused a glow into their feelings, and through their feelings into their imagination ; and again it set them upon a courageous inquisition into first principles, — first principles of politics, of morals, and of the individual life as it is connected with the life of society. They were lovers before they became thinkers, but thought was fostered by love. The object of their passion was not a single person, but society itself : —

> " Society became my glittering bride,
> And airy hopes my children."

In this passion there was, no doubt, something immature, something hectic, something turbid,

much unwise heat, not a little of illusion. It
was not all illusion; and indeed there are illusions which lead us towards the truth. In those
days, says Wordsworth, it was bliss to be alive;
the bliss was composed of a boundless hope, an
unqualified faith, and a faith and hope which
seemed to be one with charity for all mankind.
This glow of spirit could not contract itself
within a defined area; like flame, it leaped the
bounds of political affairs, and passed into every
mansion of the spirit, even into every habitation
of dreams. In its direct and immediate influence the genius of the Revolution did an injury
to art; it tended to convert the poet into a
declaimer, a preacher, the missionary of an ill-
considered evangel. In its remoter effects the
gain was real and great. Audacities of the
imagination became easy and natural, which
twenty years previously had been impossible,
or, at best, would have resulted in strain and
spasm. Such a vast exploration of the individual
mind and of the life of society as Wordsworth
intended in his unfinished poem "The Recluse"
(of which "The Prelude" and "The Excursion"
are but fragments) might never have been conceived were it not that the deep and generous
excitement of the time had aroused every faculty

and helped to fuse all his powers into one glowing
mass, —

> "Urania, I shall need
> Thy guidance, or a greater Muse, if such
> Descend to earth or dwell in highest heaven !
> For I must tread on shadowy ground, must sink
> Deep — and aloft ascending breathe in worlds
> To which the heaven of heavens is but a veil."

Such wide-orbing speculations, or shadows and
phantasms of speculation, as were set in motion
by Coleridge's brain derived their existence from
those passions which roused his intellect to seek
out general principles as the explanation and
justification of his hopes and fears. Such bold
acquisition and skilful arrangement of masses of
material as are seen in Southey's series of narrative poems, illustrating the religions of the world,
Mohammedan, Hindoo, Christian, came only in
part from his native alertness and energy of
mind ; that energy was in large part infused into
him by the emotional excitement of the time,
which entering his spirit passed from the sphere
of political interests to the region of the imagination. In times of ease we steer our way by a
little watchfulness and dexterity, a gentle shift-
ing of the helm to right or left; but when the
storm is up, we have larger problems to consider.
With minds such as Southey's, minds which were

not endowed with any high gift of speculation, the influence of the Revolution was in the main an affair of the heart, an affair of sentiment. With Wordsworth and Coleridge, who followed ideas and created new combinations of thought and feeling, the intellectual influence, if not primary, was of equal power with that which aroused the passions. They could not feel strongly without seeking to establish their feelings upon a basis of thought. The principles of society, the laws of the individual mind, became with them the subjects of studious meditation. But because their whole nature was aroused, they could not conduct their study of first principles by the understanding alone; feelings and imagination must needs co-operate with the understanding. They were thinkers, but of the emotional and imaginative, not of the ratiocinative, order. And their inquisition into first principles extended beyond politics and morals, to religion, to art, to literature. Such a research for the foundations of belief and of opinion underlies much of Wordsworth's poetry ; it directed and controlled all the later work of Coleridge.

Add to this another important influence on literature proceeding from the great series of events connected with the Revolution. This

stupendous epic of history arrived at a moment
when the Romantic revival was in full progress.
In Germany, in France, in England, the Romantic
movement was characterized by an immense development in literature of the personal, the individual factor.   It was in large measure a
translation of the principle of individualism into
art.   The literature of the classical period in
France, the literature of the age of Louis XIV.,
had been eminently social.   It rested upon a
broad community of thought and of sentiment
existing between the writers of the time and
the audience which they addressed.   Hence,
while it was distinguished in the region of
oratory, in the eloquence of public satire, the
eloquence of great preachers, the magnificent
rhetoric of the stage, there was almost a total
absence of the lyrical element, the cry of individual passion.   Even the majestic choruses of
" Athalie " are the expression, not of private, but
of public passion.   Even the exquisite sentiment
of La Fontaine's Fables is a sentiment which
arises from a common *bonhomie* and an average
good sense.   The same general statement is true
of English literature of the age of Queen Anne.
It was eminently social, and this social quality
is its highest characteristic.   The poets and

essayists endeavored to say what was known to all, what was felt by all, what would be at once accepted by all, but what had never before been so happily expressed. And, accordingly, lyrical poetry languished in what is called our Augustan age. The Romantic movement, on the contrary, was an assertion of the *ego*. The individual, private passion of a Saint Preux, of a Werther, claimed its rights, and declared that all men must accept it, even in its excess, with sympathetic interest. The closing years of the eighteenth century and the opening years of the nineteenth, with Burns and Blake, Coleridge and Keats, Byron and Shelley, are pre-eminent for the keenness and the intensity of the lyrical cry in literature. A vast epic, however, of historical struggle, of national aspiration and national effort, was being unrolled before the eyes of men. It did not stifle the lyrical cry of the Romantic poets, but it added a breadth and volume to their passions. It lifted Byron out of his egoism. It made Shelley look from cloudland to the earth. Eminent poets Byron and Shelley must have been in any age; but in an age of tranquillity their poetry would have lost half its motive power. We might have had an " Epipsychidion," a " Sensitive Plant," a " Skylark," an " Elegy on

Thyrza," or such a lyric romance as "When we two parted;" assuredly we should never have had a "Prometheus Unbound," an "Ode to Liberty," a "Prophecy of Dante," or a "Childe Harold."

One of the chief interests of a critic in studying the literature of this extraordinary epoch lies in the effort which he is called on to make in order to disentangle the various influences which became formative in the work of each eminent writer of the time.   We have seen how the spirit of the Evangelical Revival, the new warmth of religious feeling, was united in the poetry of Cowper with the philanthropic or humanitarian sentiment of his age, and with the Revolutionary tendency towards simplification.   Through Burns the old stream of Scottish song flowed into the new enthusiasm of the Revolution with its aspiration towards equality.   Both Coleridge and Southey belonged to the Romantic movement: the latter accepting it in its more obvious aspects, but allying romance with a noble, ethical feeling; the former refining romance through the rare delicacy of his imagination.   Both were affected by the sentimentality of the second half of the eighteenth century; but Southey, in his early years, in a far greater degree than Coleridge, partly because he was less interested in general ideas, partly because he was less remote in the processes of his imagination from real life, from the ways and works of men, and had a more direct sympathy with the sorrows of the outcast and the down-trodden. Coleridge, on the other hand, was influenced far more than Southey by the philosophical transcendentalism of the age, that new turn of speculation, accompanied by a corresponding movement of the feelings and the imagination, which found a Divine Presence immanent in all the operations of nature and in all the evolving changes of human society.

Southey's literary activity was much greater than that of either Wordsworth or Coleridge. By the close of the century his published work far exceeded in quantity that of either of his friends. It was his merit to have his faculties well in hand; he did not brood and contemplate, like Wordsworth ; he did not dream and loiter, like Coleridge. He was ambitious of achievement; he accumulated and arranged; he taxed his nerve and his invention; he was on the way to become a skilled literary craftsman. His was a high-strung nature, full of nervous energy, alert and sensitive. I have elsewhere described him — and the words are not inappropriate — as an Arab steed doing the work of a pack-horse. "How has this man," asked Carlyle, when he met Southey in 1836, or a year later, " contrived, with such a nervous system, to keep alive for near sixty years ? Now blushing under his gray hairs, rosy like a maiden of fifteen; now slaty almost, like a rattlesnake or fiery serpent ? How has he not been torn to pieces long since, under such furious pulling this way and that ? He must have somewhere a great deal of methodic virtue in him; I suppose, too, his heart is thoroughly honest, which helps considerably ! " His heart was, indeed, what Carlyle supposed it. And he brought to literature something which controlled his excessive sensibility, — a certain Stoicism, increased by his devotion to Epictetus, an ardent admiration for heroic character in man and woman, and a finely poised will. He toiled among books; the accumulated possessions of his intellect balanced, and sometimes more than balanced, his inborn powers. Yet, in general, before the material which he had acquired left his mind, it had received the peculiar impress of his individuality.

The Revolution reached him early ; a sanguine temperament predisposed him to accept its radiant promises; it announced new heroisms,

and his heart was high-mettled. He accepted
the political doctrine *en bloc*. " I read and all
but worshipped Godwin," he says; yet he remained essentially idealistic, and at no time
was attracted by the materialistic teaching of
French eighteenth-century philosophy, from
which Godwin had derived much. " In my
youth," he wrote, " when my stock of knowledge
consisted of such an acquaintance with Greek
and Roman history as is acquired in the course
of a regular scholastic education, when my heart
was full of poetry and romance, and Lucan and
Akenside were at my tongue's end, I fell into the
political opinions which the French Revolution
was then scattering throughout Europe; and following those opinions with ardor wherever they
led, I soon perceived that inequalities of rank
were a light evil compared to the inequalities
of property, and those more fearful distinctions
which the want of moral and intellectual culture
occasion between man and man. At that time,
and with those opinions, or rather feelings (for
their root was in the heart and not in the understanding), I wrote 'Wat Tyler,' as one who was
impatient of 'all the oppressions that are done
under the sun.' "

" Wat Tyler " may serve to warn any young

poet of the dangers of making his art a direct
vehicle for political doctrine. It transfers to
dramatis personæ of the fourteenth century, in
almost a crude form, the Revolutionary sentiments and Revolutionary rhetoric of the writer's
own day. While his daughter and her lover
dance gayly around the maypole, Tyler, the Dept-
ford blacksmith, looks on with a brow of gloom.
All his life he has been a staid, hard-working
man, —

> " Up with the lark at labor — sober — honest —
> Of an unblemish'd character."

It is bitterness to his soul to reflect that the
fruit of his toil amounts to the six groats which
are presently to be claimed by the tax-gatherer.
And for what ? To massacre the French (as in
Southey's own day), to murder men he had never
seen ! When Tyler has avenged the insult
offered to his child, and the mob assemble with
cries of " Liberty ! liberty ! no war ! " the task
awaits them of delivering from prison the virtuous and benevolent priest, John Ball, whose
lessons to his flock have been learnt from Dr.
Priestley and Dr. Price, with occasional lectures
from William Godwin. The Archbishop of Can-
terbury, a melancholy contrast to the priest of
the people, urges that King Richard should meet

the rebels, concede all their demands, swearing in
their presence a solemn oath, from which he shall
be afterwards duly absolved, while, at the moment, the royal troops gather around to capture
or to slay the ringleaders. Tyler is stabbed from
behind as he pleads for the rights of the sovereign people. A mock trial is reserved for Ball,
who announces, in presence of the king and
nobles, the evangel of equality, prophesies the
time when those truths for which he is about to
suffer shall be confessed by all men, and calmed
by his vision of the future receives from Sir John
Tresilian's lips the sentence that he shall suffer
the utmost penalties of the law. Southey's dramatic sketch was a hasty product of his twentieth
year; there is nothing in it to dishonor his
heart, and at twenty it is no disgrace to be
neither a thinker nor a dramatic craftsman.

Southey's sympathies went with the Girondist
party. Their successors in power he looked on
as wretches who only masked their criminal instincts under the name of Republican. He remained for a time true to his democratic faith,
but he began to despair of the Revolution. In
the tenth book of "The Prelude" Wordsworth
has told of the transport that seized him, the deep
gratitude he rendered to eternal Justice, when on

a summer day of 1794 in crossing the Ulverston
Sands the words suddenly reached him, " Robespierre is dead!" The tragic incidents of that
event were hastily thrown into a miniature
drama, almost as the newspapers had arrived, by
Southey and Coleridge. On its publication at
Cambridge the name of Coleridge alone, who contributed the first act, was connected with it.
"The Fall of Robespierre," with one moment of
relief where Adelaide sings her song of domestic
peace to Tallien, the Mark Antony of the plot, is
a tumult of conflicting parties and leaders, in
which the action is heavily draped in voluminous
and turbid rhetoric. Contemporary passions and
events will not pass into art by the short and
easy method of transposing the journals into
blank verse. Poetry must be truer than history
or it has no right to exist.

"Wat Tyler" and "The Fall of Robespierre"
were mere adventures or escapades. Southey's
"Joan of Arc" was an achievement of strenuous
ambition. Crude and feeble as many of its pages
are, the poem has in it the glow and ardor of the
time. A period of great public events had roused
the young writer's imagination, and had given
breadth and energy to its movement. In the late
summer and early autumn of 1793 Southey's epic

was written with enthusiasm, and with the speed that enthusiasm begets. Towards the close of the following year it was announced for publication by Joseph Cottle, the young publisher of Bristol, who was almost as ardent and quite as inexperienced as Southey himself. While the printing proceeded, the poem was recast and recomposed, and a considerable contribution for the second book was received from Coleridge. At a later date Southey, who had a certain regard for his first important contribution to literature, rehandled his text; to know the spirit in which he originally wrote, to make acquaintance with the work which Lamb, in his callow days of criticism, declared sufficient to redeem the character of the age from the imputation of degenerating in poetry, we must read the epic in the original quarto of 1796, as issued from a Bristol press.

"Joan of Arc" is romantic; it is sentimental; it is revolutionary. Three streams of contemporary influence met in its turbid tide. The poem attempts to revive the pomp and splendor of mediæval court and camp and consistory; the besieged fortress, the cathedral, rich with many-colored lights, rise as the new stage-properties of the imagination; the king, the warrior, the priest, pass across the scene. The supernatural effects are duly introduced; by strange and miraculous attestations the mission of the Maid is confirmed; in awful vision she is led through scenes of horror which to Taylor of Norwich seemed to rival those of Dante's "Inferno." The poem is also in the vein of eighteenth-century sentiment. When in 1814 Coleridge turned back to its pages, in which was embedded a portion of his own early work, he was astonished at "the transmogrification of the fanatic virago into a modern novel-pawing proselyte of the Age of Reason, a Tom Paine in petticoats, but so lovely! and in love so dear!" It had been nearer the mark if instead of a Tom Paine in petticoats Coleridge had said a Mary Wollstonecraft in armor. At the call of her country the Maid of Orleans, an amorous shepherdess, abandons love, or rather exalts it into a lofty, protective friendship. Her lover, Theodore, dies, but his spirit watches and assists her from the heights of heaven. There are frequent outbreaks of emotion, which it would be unjust to characterize as sentimental, over the wrongs and griefs of rural France, the daughter weeping for her father, the maiden bewailing her betrothed, the starving peasant, the desolated homestead, — ill fruits of a war of ambition. The epic, in the third place, is revolutionary. The heroine is an offspring

of the people.   The monarch, for whose cause she
abandons peace and love, is a luxurious wanton,
who can be roused from his sloth and shame only
through the spiritual influence and authority of
this virgin child of nature.   The courtiers at
Paris are given over to lordly riot.   The doctors
of theology are slaves of bigotry and superstition,
as cruel as ignorant.   Before them stands Joan,—
her cheek suffused with the loveliest blush, her
dark hair waving in the wind, her figure bending
lightly like a snowdrop in the waste.   Interro-
gated by the stern ecclesiastics as to her faith in
Holy Church, she answers as a docile pupil of
Rousseau's Savoyard Vicar, —

> "'T was Nature taught my early youth
> Religion. . . . Nature bade me see the God
> Confest in all that lives, and moves, and is.
> . . . .
> It is not Nature that can teach to sin:
> Nature is all Benevolence — all Love,
> All Beauty."

In the somewhat appalling allegory of the
ninth book ("the finest in the volume," according
to Lamb, in the manner he conceived of Dante
or Ariosto, writers still unknown to him), the
spirit of Theodore describes the primitive age of
love and happiness, before gold was known or
private property existed, — such a blissful state

as the young Pantisocrats had hoped to revive on
the banks of the Susquehanna; from which
retrospect the seer rises to a prophecy of the
coming era of universal happiness and freedom,
when

> "Oppression shall be chained, and Poverty
> Die, and, with her, the Brood of Miseries;
> And Virtue and Equality preserve
> The reign of Love, and Earth shall once again
> Be Paradise, whilst Wisdom shall secure
> The state of bliss which Ignorance betrayed."

Southey's epic closes with the coronation of
Charles at Rheims, accompanied by admonish-
ment from the peasant Maid, to whom he owes
his crown, that he should be no common tyrant,
but the true Father of his People.

Southey's volume of minor Poems, published
in 1797, and a second volume which appeared
two years later, were written in the humanitarian
spirit of the time; many of the pieces are rillets
of Revolutionary sensibility. The principal
poem, "The Triumph of Woman," is dedicated
to Mary Wollstonecraft. Several sonnets deal
with various aspects of Slavery; an ode is
addressed to the Genius of Africa; a ballad
records the dying confession of crime uttered
by a sailor who had aided in the iniquities of the

slave-trade. In the earlier of the volumes things as they are in so-called civilized society are studied in a series of Eclogues, of which the scene is the convict settlement at Botany Bay. Elinor has been the victim of brutal passions; exhausted with famine, she had been guilty of some petty theft; now she is an outcast from humanity. William had been a happy rustic in a home of innocence and peace, until he dared to direct his gun against the squire's game that devoured the seed of his fields. Humphrey had been tempted by the red-coats to forsake his plough, and when turned adrift had sunk to misery and crime. John had been seized by a press-gang, and, lustily resisting, was wounded, and, wounded, was driven to disgrace by want. If each warred with the world, had not the world first unjustly warred with each? "Why do the poor complain?" asks the rich man in another poem; the poet replies by leading him through the frozen streets, where the aged mendicant wanders forlorn, and the child seeks bread for a dying father, and the soldier's wife is begging her way back to her parish, and the flaunting girl resorts to the most wretched relief from her distress. Some unrhymed dactylic stanzas (in which Coleridge assisted) describe a woe-

begone mother, whose husband has perished in
the wars; some sapphics tell of a wretched
night-wanderer on the heath, who appeals vainly
for pity to the occupants of a passing chariot,
and who is found cold and dead when morning
breaks. Of a series of Inscriptions, one for a cen-
otaph at Ermenonville does honor to Rousseau;
one for a monument in the New Forest tells of
the cruelties of the first Anglo-Norman King;
one for a column at Newbury laments the deaths
of the patriots Falkland and Hampden; one written for an apartment in Chepstow Castle recalls
its glory and shame as the place of a Regicide's
imprisonment, —

> " Dost thou ask his crime?
> He had rebelled against the King, and sat
> In judgment on him; for his ardent mind
> Shaped goodliest plans of happiness on earth,
> And peace and liberty. Wild dreams! But such
> As Plato loved; such as with holy zeal
> Our Milton worshipped. Blessed hopes! awhile
> From man withheld, even to the latter days
> When Christ shall come, and all things be fulfilled."

It is obvious that Southey's revolutionary
ardor, as he himself said, was more of the heart
than of the understanding. He did his cause
some wrong by seeming to push the trade of
poetical pity too importunately. Yet his indict-

ment of society was not without a warrant in facts; he did not stay to theorize; he derived sufficient impulses for song from his keen sensibility to human suffering, from the stoicism which was the counterpoise to his sensibility, and from those imaginative hopes which pointed to a better, purer, and happier condition of society as the result of some momentous change in the established order of things.

Coleridge from the first contemplated the French Revolution more as a thinker, and, though he embraced some of Godwin's opinions and among them the determinism of Godwin, as a religious thinker. The idea of God possessed him; he seemed to feel the Divine Presence as a breeze, plastic and vast, which plays over and through the whole of animated nature like the wind amid the chords of an æolian harp. True freedom was to be found in communion and co-operancy with this universal Deity; to chain down one's thoughts in false philosophy to the gross and visible sphere, — that indeed was slavery. Through the fierce strife between the powers of chaos and the powers of order which fills the world there is yet discernible to the eye of faith an eternal process of good. In this religious optimism, this belief of a divine evolution of society, unhasting, unresting, lay in embryo the future conservatism of Coleridge. His contribution to "Joan of Arc," afterwards enlarged by the writer and printed among his own poems under the title "The Destiny of Nations," closes with an address to the Father of Earth and Heaven, —

> "All-conscious Presence of the Universe!
> Nature's vast ever-acting Energy!" —

which operates alike through the prophet's lonely voice and the frenzy of the people. Godwin, an optimist of the Reason, viewed with indignant scorn the superstitions of the past as deadliest foes to human progress. To Coleridge they appeared to be a fragment of the eternal process of the truth, —

> "Wild phantasies! yet wise,
> On the victorious goodness of high God
> Teaching reliance, and medicinal hope,
> Till from Bethabra northward, heavenly Truth
> With gradual steps, winning her difficult way,
> Transfer their rude Faith perfected and pure."

"Religious Musings," which as a completed poem its author antedated when he stated that it was written on the Christmas Eve of 1794, is another vision of the destiny of nations; it might not unaptly be called Coleridge's "Queen Mab;"

but while Shelley's early poem is certainly not theistic, in the ordinary sense of that word, Coleridge's philosophy of history discovers God everywhere immanent and active. In the totality of nature lives one omnipresent Mind, whose holiest name is Love. Hence all things must work together for good, and those dread ministers that shower down vengeance on these latter days have yet filled their vials with salutary wrath. To annihilate self in the exclusive consciousness of God is to become one with the highest order and the purest freedom; to lose the sense of God is to lose our centre, it is to throw ourselves out of the moral cohesion of the world, and to pass into a spiritual anarchy. Before the final victory of God and his Christ, offences must needs come; and the capital offence of his own day Coleridge found in the war of banded despots against the French Republic. He looks back to the primeval age of innocence — the favorite Revolutionary fiction — and traces the commencement of property as a source both of evil and of good. Coleridge does not declare himself against civilization, as such, nor against the arts of civilization. As in "Joan" he maintains that superstitions lead towards truth, so here he urges that wealth and luxury, demanding new forms of beauty in music, painting, architecture, decorative design, tend at last by sensual wants to unsensualize the mind, which finds the best delight of art, not in lethargy or mere possessions, but in its own activity,—

"From Avarice thus, from Luxury and War,
  Sprang heavenly Science, and from Science Freedom."

He dwells on all the oppressions that are done under the sun; he remembers the tears of such as are afflicted and have no comforter; he anticipates the day of retribution as at hand. Even now the storm begins; but through evil God works out a glorious gain. Love is omnipresent, and is omnific. Life, with all its errors, is "a vision, shadowy of Truth." He foresees the blessed future, when the wondrous plan of love shall be achieved, and all God's coadjutors — Milton and Newton, Hartley, the "wisest of mortal kind," and Priestley, "patriot, saint, and sage"— shall have a part in the fulfilment of that for which they thought and hoped and toiled. "Religious Musings" impresses us now somewhat as one of the sermons, eloquent, copious, sanguine, preached by Coleridge from a Unitarian pulpit. To Lamb the poem seemed to be more than worthy of Milton.

In the Bristol addresses, delivered by Coleridge while he was still almost a youth, he describes the several types of erring or imperfect patriots, — those who are without principles, and vary in their opinions with every wind of rumor from France; those who drink in the inflammatory harangues of some enthusiast, taking poison for food and rage for liberty; those who would pull down but care not to build up. He proceeds to contrast with these the thoughtful and disinterested patriot,— him with whom the sympathetic passions have become irresistible habits, rendering duty a necessity and a part of genuine self-interest. Such a lover of human welfare has come to regard all the affairs of men as a process; he never hurries and never pauses; he advances in no dim twilight of political knowledge, but steadfastly presses forward on an opening scene, beholding in clear illumination a vast and varied landscape of existence. At a later date Coleridge declared that, ardent as had been his Republican faith, deep as had been his indignation against those two massive pillars of Oppression, as he styles them, monarchy and aristocracy, he had never been a convert to Jacobinism in politics. But what is Jacobinism? A system of thought, Coleridge answers, which denies all rightful

origin to government except so far as it is de-
rivable from principles contained in human reason, and at the same time denies all truth and
distinct meaning to the words *right* and *duty* by
affirming that the human mind consists of nothing but manifold modifications of passive sen-
sation.   Coleridge's faith in a Divine energy
working in and through mundane affairs predisposed him to seek and to find a certain latent
truth in all wide-spread institutions and long-
established customs.   Yet no one desired more
ardently than he, in the days of Aspheterism and
Pantisocracy, a remodelling of social life under
more favorable conditions than were possible in
old civilizations which rest upon the basis of
private property.   No one in after years could
better understand the errors of generous youth
or early manhood, enamoured of a system which
seems to combine "at once the austere beauty of
science with all the lights and colors of imagination, and with all the warmth of wide religious
charity," while in fact it may be no other than
the disguised emissary of moral anarchy and
political despotism.

What remained with Southey, what with Coleridge from their early Revolutionary faith and
fervor ?   Both passed over to the opposite camp,

to the party of conservation. It was common in their own day to represent them as apostates from their creed, as faint-hearted or self-interested alarmists, who had forsaken their first love. But it almost always happens that a convert carries much of his former temper and habits of mind into any new faith which he may accept. If we look beneath the surface to essentials, we shall find that any breach of continuity in the course of their thought was less violent and less complete than it has been often represented. Neither Southey nor Coleridge was conscious of a betrayal of principle ; neither would admit that he had hastily fled from the position which he originally occupied.

The Revolutionary zeal of Southey was chiefly distinguished by its humanitarian complexion. He looked upon the Revolution as the armed champion of the suffering, the weak, the poor, the injured, the downtrodden. The progress of events led him to the conclusion that the Revolution, as conducted by its leaders, did not make for human happiness. He came to believe that under the existing constitution of England the rights of the people might be better safeguarded than they could be if all that had grown up and was established were to be flung into the crucible. He came to regard the English Church as a great organization which held a trust for the good of the nation. But he still ardently desired the improvement of the world; "there is no opinion from which I should so hardly be driven and so reluctantly part," he wrote in 1829, "as the belief that the world will continue to improve, even as it has hitherto been continually improving." He still saw abundant need for reform and amendment; he still devoted a large portion of his time and thought to the cause of reformation. The ghostly Sir Thomas More of Southey's "Colloquies" fears that his interlocutor is still in Utopia, because he viewed with so much favor the industrial schemes of Robert Owen of Lanark. Southey cannot be called an original thinker in any eminent sense of that word. The historical feeling was strong within him. It was natural for him, constituted as he was (and perhaps it was wise as well as natural), to accept the framework of things as it had been slowly built up by history; but he held that without shaking that framework much might be done to render life better for England of the nineteenth century. He pleaded for national education as the first and greatest need of the people; and he maintained that the Church

of England was so organized that with quickened
and well-directed energy it might become the
chief agent in national education. He anticipated
a time when landed property might be held, not
in the hands of a few great territorial owners,
but by those who themselves ploughed the field
and gathered the harvest. He urged the need
and duty of the diffusion of good and cheap
literature. He desired some well-organized system of colonization, as a gain both to those who
fared abroad and those who remained in their
native land. Among other reforms advocated
by the Tory Quarterly Reviewer were a wholesome training for the children of misery and vice
in great cities; the establishment of Protestant
sisters of charity and a better order of hospital
nurses; the establishment of savings' banks in
all small towns ; the abolition of flogging in the
army and navy, except in extreme cases; improvements in the poor laws ; alterations in the
game laws ; alterations in the criminal laws, with
a view to restricting the punishment of death
to great offences ; the execution of criminals
within prison walls ; alterations in the factory
system for the benefit of the operative, and
especially as to the employment of children ;
national works to be undertaken in times of dis-

tress; the employment of paupers in reclaiming waste lands; the cessation of interments in crowded cities; the commutation of tithes; an increased number of clergymen, of colleges, and of courts of law that a speedier administration of justice might be secured.[1] Many of these proposals of the Reformer Southey have since been carried into effect.

The work of Coleridge was different; it was the work of a thinker, and in a certain sense of a Revolutionary thinker. He, like Southey, accepted the existing framework of society, but, with that ardent spirit of research for first principles, derived in large measure from the passionate interest which he took in politics and morals, when he planned his Pantisocracy, he bent his mind to ascertain the *idea* of each existing institution and established form of thought, — the *idea*, which had been overlaid and obscured by the accretion of circumstance; and thus he endeavored to effect a new interpretation of accepted things. This, indeed, was to aim at a revolution in some respects more profound and more far-reaching in its consequences than any merely external dis-

[1] In the above I recite, as in my Life of Southey ("English Men of Letters"), pp. 154, 155, from a list drawn up by Southey's son.

turbance of the arrangements of society. He
cannot be said to have propounded a complete
and coherent system of philosophy, but he led
men to inquire into the meaning of what they
professed to believe, with a result which was
alarming to many, and to others was like the awakening from dreams to reality. In metaphysical
speculation, in ethics, in politics, in theology, in
Biblical criticism, in the criticism of literature, he
suggested a new exposition of received formulas.
He quickened the sense of religion by reducing
or attempting to reduce dogma, imposed from
without, to facts of the spiritual consciousness
and their inner significance. He would preserve
the national Church, but he conceived the national
Church not as the mere Anglican ecclesiastical
system; he conceived it somewhat in the manner
of the great seventeenth-century revolutionist,
Milton, as the clerisy, the intellectual and spiritual incorporation of the whole people. He
honored the Bible as highly as they did who
regarded every sentence of Holy Scripture as
written by the finger of God; but for him it was
no hewn cistern of dogma and of law; it became a
living fountain of wisdom and of love. In like
manner he did not attempt to displace the old
conceptions in politics and morals, but he desired

to discover the vital centre of each conception, and to deliver this from the incrustations of custom and unilluminated tradition. If he criticised literature, he did not seek to shift the ancient landmarks or to establish any novel standard of valuation ; he penetrated to the living soul of each work of art, and gave a new meaning to the old admirations. In this effort towards a new rendering of things Coleridge was engaged in a work of revolution, but a revolution which should conserve by renewing rather than merely effect a clearance by the method of destruction. In his remarkable essay on Coleridge, Mr. Mill, writing as a radical, shows how incomplete, from his own radical standpoint, appeared the Revolutionary work of Bentham. What was lacking to Bentham and the school of Bentham was supplied, as he held, by Coleridge and by what he terms the Germano-Coleridgian school. The Conservative party, he supposed, as far as it deserves the contemptuous title of "the stupid party," was little likely to be pleased with Coleridge's later ideas. "Most of all," he declares, "ought an enlightened Radical or Liberal to rejoice over such a conservative as Coleridge." The white-haired philosopher of Highgate, if a different person from the young Pantisocrat of 1794, was at least a lineal descendant of that enthusiastic insurgent.

While the elder representatives of the Revolution and those of the party of Order met in combat, bulky pamphlet being hurled against pamphlet, the younger Revolutionary spirits were assailed by younger partisans of the opposing force, — a light-armed troop, whose weapons were darts, effectively barbed, of ridicule. From 1799 to 1801, Canning, then under-secretary of state for foreign affairs, was connected with the "Anti-Jacobin;" among the contributors were George Ellis, Hookham Frere, Lord Morpeth, Baron Macdonald, and others. Canning had been brought up among the Whig chiefs; by Fox and Sheridan he had been introduced to Devonshire House. "But the French Revolution," as Mr. Kebbel has said, "exercised the same influence on Canning as it did on many older men, hitherto the most distinguished ornaments of the Whig party, — Burke, Windham, Spencer, Lord Fitzwilliam, — and brought them over in a body to the Tory camp." The "Anti-Jacobin, or Weekly Examiner" was designed to meet the newspaper propaganda of the sympathizers with Revolution. Gifford was appointed editor, and the first number appeared in November, 1797. At the out-

set it was intended to open what the writers of
Hookham Frere's Memoirs describe as heavy
batteries of fact and argument against the enemy.
"Authentic news was to be supplied, the mis-
representations of the opposition press were to
be refuted under a regularly classified gradation
of 'Mistakes,' 'Misstatements,' and 'Lies;' and
a considerable space was to be devoted to formal
essays on historical and constitutional questions." In the Valedictory Address of the last
number, an amusing calculation is made, in
which the number of falsehoods detected is mul-
tiplied by the number of readers, taken at fifty
thousand, with the result that a grand total of
twenty-five millions represents the aggregate of
falsehoods despatched to limbo by the "Anti-
Jacobin." It was soon found that the heavy
batteries of argument were not needed in 1797
as they might have been in 1792. The Revolution had deployed its horrors; it had led to wars
of conquest which England endeavored to restrain or to repel. A light-armed guerilla attack
of satire, parody, epigram, it was believed, would
prove more effective than grave discussion; and
verse was used to wing to its mark the arrowy
ridicule. The poetry, which indeed was a feat-
ure of the Review from the first number, was in-

troduced to the readers by Canning in a preface. The "Review," we are told, desired to amuse as well as to instruct the public; but, whatever may have been the cause, not one good and true poet of sound principles and sober practice could be found. It was necessary to go for verse to the only market where it could be procured, that of the Jacobins, and humbly to imitate the wood-notes wild of the bards of freedom: "The poet in all ages has despised riches and grandeur. The Jacobin poet improves this sentiment into a hatred of the rich and the great. The poet of other times has been an enthusiast in the love of his native soil. The Jacobin poet rejects all restriction on his feelings. *His* love is enlarged and expanded so as to comprehend all human kind." The old poet sang the actions of the warrior heroes of his country in strains that made ambition virtue. The Jacobin poet is ready to celebrate the glory of French Republicans shouting victory over fallen despots; but let his own country triumph, we are then presented with "nothing but contusions and amputations, plundered peasants and deserted looms. Our poet points the thunder of his blank verse at the head of the recruiting-sergeant, or roars in dithyrambics against the lieutenants of press-gangs."

The use of such satire as that of the "Anti-Jacobin" is not to raise a laugh against the opposite party; its use is to make men reflect, to question their own passions, to scrutinize their own enthusiasms, and to reject them if they be without warrant, or maintain them if they be well founded in spite of ridicule.   Something within us checks our full sympathy with a group of young men of rank and fashion who devoted their talents to mocking all that seemed generous in feeling to men of a more sanguine temper. "Your young men," declares the prophet Joel, "shall see visions;" and even if the visions be too bright with promise, they often lead through illusions to the truth.   The brilliant young Tories of the "Anti-Jacobin" were assuredly no visionary sons of the prophets.   On the other hand, the dangers arising to England from ill-considered zeal were grave; and there is a gallantry in defensive sallies as well as in the onset of attack.   If Burke had been accused of sentimentalities, the retort was natural; there were in the opposite party spurious sentiment, hectic excitements, unreal rhetoric, extravagant dreams.   Connected with these there was a loosening of the bonds of morality and a tendency to substitute sophisticated feelings for the old plain

laws of human duty.   Against these it was well
to aim the shafts of ridicule; laughter clears
the air; there is much virtue in good sense,
and what is genuine will survive a peal of laughter.   No one can regret that the first object of
attack was Southey; his heart was essentially
sound; his morals were pure and manly; but it
is true that some of the errors of generous and
inexperienced youth were his.   The Friend of
Humanity who will see the needy knife-grinder
damned before he gives his sixpence, is no unfair
satire on the theoretic philanthropist whose eyes
are in the ends of the earth.   The Soldier's
Friend who greets the drummer-boy in Southeyan
dactylics, offering him "nice clever books by
Tom Paine," and handbills, and half-crowns to
raise a barrack mutiny, is a legitimate caricature
of the missionaries of sedition.   There was a
sufficient efflux of nonsense from the friends of
the Revolution to make the mocking chorus seem
something less than a parody, —

> "Reason, philosophy, fiddledum diddledum,
>   Peace and fraternity, higgledy piggledy,
>   Higgledy piggledy, fiddledum diddledum."

What was honorable and of permanent value
in the movement of change could not suffer by
exposure of the insincerity of its dishonest ad-

vocates or the folly of indiscreet enthusiasts; it might be trusted to prove in the end that all was not "fiddledum diddledum." Godwin and others had assailed the institution of marriage. The Anti-Jacobins hardly intensified the outcry, when, in their parody of Payne Knight's "Progress of Civil Society," they mourn over that two-headed monster formed by unnatural law, — man and wife, — and comment on the cruelty which, while the gamester in whist and cribbage may change his partner and continue his sport, compels a husband to play the long rubber of connubial failure or success with "one unceasing wife."

Sheridan, a prominent figure of the Whig party and a brilliant writer for the stage, had assisted in the translation of Kotzebue's play, "The Stranger." Many other dramas of Kotzebue, at once sentimental and revolutionary, were popular. Goethe's "Stella," with its questionable morality on the relation of the sexes, had appeared in an English garb. Replying to a letter of "Mucius" in the "Anti-Jacobin," Cato comments on the growing profligacy of manners in the Revolutionary days, "evidenced by the most frequent, flagrant, shameless, and aggravated violations of the nuptial tie." The evil was a real and present evil. Coleridge, in his "Satyrane's Letters," defined the whole system of such dramas as those of Kotzebue as "a moral and intellectual Jacobinism of the most dangerous kind;" the secret of their popularity lay in "the confusion and subversion of the natural order of things, their causes and their effects; in the excitement of surprise by representing the qualities of liberality, refined feeling, and a nice sense of honor in persons and in classes of life where experience teaches us least to expect them; and in rewarding with all the sympathies that are the dues of virtue those criminals whom law, reason, and religion have excommunicated from our esteem." The words of a critic or a moralist might have had inattentive hearers; but laughter became an irresistible moralist, when the imagined Mr. Higgins of the "Anti-Jacobin" united the plots of "Stella" and "The Stranger" in his romantic historical drama "The Rovers." "If the play has a proper run," wrote the extraordinary and indefatigable Higgins, "it will, I think, do much to unhinge the present notions of men with regard to the obligations of civil society, and to substitute, in lieu of a sober contentment, and regular discharge of the duties incident to each man's particular situation, a wild

desire of undefinable latitude and extravagance
. . . it will do much to set men about doing what
they like, where they like, when they like, and how
they like." The heroine of "The Rovers," Matilda Pottingen, had been first seen by her lover
Casimire — a lover already wedded — in a peasant's cabin, employed, like the Lotte of Werther,
in "spreading bread and butter for the children,
in a light-blue riding-habit." Among the *dramatis personæ* are Pantalowsky and Britchinda,
children of Matilda by Casimire; Joachim, Jabel,
and Amarantha, children of Matilda by Rogero;
the children of Casimire and Cecilia, with their respective nurses; and "several children, — fathers
and mothers unknown." Rogero, the hero, lan-
guishes in a dungeon, the victim of ecclesiastical
tyranny; the English nobles, Beefington and
Puddingfield, are *émigrés*, who have fled from the
oppression of their country; a Knight Templar
has forsaken his dignities and embraced the
position of a waiter; an Austrian and a Prussian
grenadier have abjured their national enmity,
and have sworn to fight henceforth in the cause
of freedom. "The Rovers" is a brilliant amal-
gam of absurdities, in which not only the
Revolutionary passion of the time, but also its
overwrought sentimentality and its taste for ro-

mantic horrors are satirized, and mutually aid in heightening the effect of the whole.

For the final number of their periodical, Canning and his friends reserved the heaviest blow. The poem "New Morality" is written in the form so well adapted for epigrammatic satire, the rhymed decasyllabic couplet. The several powers of Revolutionary thought and feeling are personified in the manner of the eighteenth-century imagination, and pass in review. First, Philanthropy, not the philanthropy that dries the orphan's tears and consoles the weeping widow, but French philanthropy, which glows with the general love of all mankind, and makes its votary a friend of every country except his own. Next, Sensibility, the child of sickly Fancy, borne by Rousseau from France to Alpine solitudes : —

> "Taught by nice scale to mete her feelings strong,
> False by degrees, and exquisitely wrong:
> For the crush'd beetle *first*, — the widow'd dove,
> And all the warbled sorrows of the grove ;
> *Next* for poor suff'ring *Guilt;* and *last* of all,
> For parents, friends, a king and country's fall."

Then, Justice ; not she who tediously dangles the balance in British courts of law, but Justice holding a blood-stained book, inscribed with one sole decree of freedom for the people : —

"Free! by what means? — by folly, madness, guilt,
  By boundless rapines, blood in oceans spilt;
  By confiscation, in whose sweeping toils
  The poor man's pittance with the rich man's spoils,
  Mix'd in one common mass are swept away,
  To glut the short-liv'd tyrant of the day."

Last, Candor; who will not condemn or praise by wholesale, but loves to see-saw between right and wrong, —

" Convinced that *all* men's *motives* are the same;
  And finds, with keen discriminating sight,
  Black 's not *so* black ; — nor white *so very* white."

The moral of the whole is plain, — let the men of England guard their own hearts; let them hold by the ancient manners and ancient morals. So, and so alone, may the storm be braved; so, perhaps, in some happier hour may England become the refuge of Europe.

Such is the spirit of the "Anti-Jacobin." The writers could justly assert that it had served their purpose. It has been said that the publication was discontinued at the direct instance of Pitt, who apprehended that satire might in the end prove an unruly ally of the party.

V

RECOVERY AND REACTION: WORDS-
WORTH AND HIS FRIENDS

V

RECOVERY AND REACTION

No one among his contemporaries was more deeply moved than was Wordsworth by the great events in France. The character of his mind fitted him in a peculiar degree for receiving the full influence of the French Revolution; the circumstances of his early life brought him near the vortex of the maelstrom; and that truth to his highest self, which it was a part of his very existence to retain, — that natural piety which bound his days each to each, — made it impossible that he should ever fling away from him as a worthless illusion the hopes and aspirations of his youth. Some readers of Wordsworth are misled in their judgment of the poet by the vulgar error that he was before all else tranquil, mild, gentle, an amiable pastoral spirit. He sang of the daisy and the celandine, the linnet and the lamb; and therefore he must have been always a serene, tender, benign contemplator of things that make for peace. There can be no greater mistake; at the heart of his peace was passion; his benignity was like the greensward upon a rocky hillside. As a boy, Wordsworth was violent and moody; in his early manhood he was stern, bold, worn by exhausting ardors. De Quincey observed that "the secret fire of a temperament too fervid" caused him to look older than his years. Above all, he was strong; and what disguises this fact from careless eyes is that Wordsworth's strength did not lie in a single part or province of his nature, that he brought his several powers into harmonious action, and that each power served to balance the others. Senses, intellect, emotions, imagination, conscience, will, were all of unusual vigor; but each helped the other, each controlled the other, each was to the other an impulse and a law. And thus an equilibrium was gained, resulting from a massive harmony of powers too commonly found among men of genius arrayed against one another in dangerous conflict. His senses were of unusual keenness; his eye lived on forms and colors, on light and shadow; his ear caught the finest differences of all homeless, wandering sounds; but the senses did not war against the spirit; they were auxiliar to higher powers, serving as scouts and intelligencers of the soul. His passions were of ample volume and of persistent force; indignation, wrath, stern joy, deep fears, boundless hopes, possessed him; but these were brought into the bondage of conscience, and became the ministers of love. His imaginative fervor again and again exhausted his physical strength; but the creative mood was balanced by a mood of wise passiveness; it was not the way with his imagination to start forth, as Shelley's imagination did, to create a world of its own upon some swift suggestion of beauty or delight; it rested on reality, brooded upon reality, coalesced with it, interpreted it. His visions and his desires were captured by his intellect, and were made substantial by a moral wisdom infused into them. His intellect did not operate singly and apart, but was vitalized by his passions. If he loved freedom with all the ardor of his soul, he loved order as well. If he hoped for the future with an indefatigable hope, he also reverenced the past. His will applied itself consciously and deliberately to the task of organizing his various faculties and supporting them in their allotted task during all the years of his self-dedication to the life poetic. Each power of his nature lived in and through every other power, and in the massive equilibrium which was the result, strength was masked by strength. And thus, having first effected an inward conciliation of the jarring elements of our humanity, he was enabled to become a reconciler for his age.

The Revolution captured Wordsworth slowly and by degrees. The year 1789, which inflamed so many hearts and imaginations in England, left him almost untouched. The awakening in France seemed to him only like any other process of nature, — a renovation, indeed, but one which might be accepted without a shock. The doctrine, the passions, the rhetoric of Revolution were borne past him like voices on the wind; he heard them without fear, but they did not sink deep into his heart. He was occupied with his studious research into the poetical appearances of external nature; and the affairs of men held a secondary place in his thoughts. It was not until his residence in France, from November, 1791, to December, 1792, that he came into veritable contact with the Revolution, and even then not during the earlier weeks of his stay at Orleans. At first he consorted with military men of the Royalist party. As yet, Wordsworth understood little of the condition of society or of the course of events which led up to the Revolution; but the aristocratic prejudices of his companions quickened the Republican spirit within him. When, a little later, he gained the friendship of the patriot-soldier, Michel Beaupuy, the democratic faiths and hopes and charities which dwelt half unawares in his heart were brought into the light of consciousness, and for the first time he became an ardent champion of the new cause. Beaupuy was fifteen years older than his young English friend; he was of most engaging person, a thinker as well as a soldier, a man of the purest morals, one who had something of antique virtue united with a modern enthusiasm, one to whom the humanitarian beliefs had the force of a religion. Wordsworth's early love-making with nature was succeeded by a love-making with society. His conversion was not the effect merely of theory, or of declamation, or of sentimental musings on the sorrows of mankind; it was the fruit of an experience, and it tended not towards rhetoric, but towards action. When, in October, 1792, he visited Paris, the massacres of September were recent; he felt the ground rocking with earthquake beneath his feet; and had the opportunity occurred, he was prepared to risk his life for the future hopes of France. Happily, circumstances recalled him to England; happily, he did not forfeit his true mission by becoming an orator of the Convention; but there was a moment when he supposed it possible that he might have devoted his life to the political service of the country through whose conduct, amid appalling dangers, he believed that the destiny of mankind was put to stake.

In 1793 he wrote his prose apology for the French Revolution, a long letter addressed to Watson, Bishop of Llandaff, and evidently designed for publication as a pamphlet. It is remarkable for its sternness and the fervor of its faith. Wordsworth justifies the execution of Louis XVI., and would reserve the passion of pity for worthier objects than a fallen king. He acknowledges the sanguinary violence of the Revolution, but pleads that a time of revolution cannot be the season of true liberty. He rejoices in the confiscation of ecclesiastical property. He maintains the superiority of the Republican to other forms of government, on the ground that it identifies the interests of the governors with those of the governed. He argues on behalf of the reduction of the inequalities among citizens to those inevitable inequalities which government by representation involves. He points out the urgent need of Parliamentary reform in

England.   When, in the same year, war between
France and England was declared, Wordsworth's
nature underwent the most violent strain that it
had ever experienced.   He loved his native land;
yet he could wish for nothing but disaster to her
arms.   His feelings were, as he says, " soured and
corrupted."   As the days passed, he found it
more and more difficult to sustain his faith in
the Revolution; first, he abandoned belief in the
leaders, but he still trusted in the people; then
the people seemed to have grown insane with
the intoxication of blood.   France attacked her
neighbors in aggressive wars; she had become
Europe's chief offender.   Wordsworth was driven
back from his defence of the Revolution, in its
historical development, to a bare faith in the
abstract idea.   He clung to theories; the free
and joyous movement of his sympathies ceased;
opinions stifled the spontaneous life of the spirit;
these opinions were tested and re-tested by the
intellect, till, in the end, exhausted by inward
debate, he yielded up moral questions in despair.

It was no sudden collapse of a rash enthusiasm.   The strands of a cable which seemed to
hold him at anchorage were severed painfully
and one by one.   The alteration ultimately effected in his mind went far deeper than the

region of political opinions. In his effort to maintain his faith in the doctrine of the Revolution by the sole aid of the reason, Wordsworth was acting in opposition to what was deepest in his nature. Doubtless at this time Godwin was the master of his mind; but by processes of the understanding alone Wordsworth could attain no vital body of truth. Rather he felt that things of far more worth than political opinions — natural instincts, sympathies, passions, intuitions — were being disintegrated or denaturalized. The tragedy of "The Borderers," if it possesses no high dramatic value, is of much autobiographic importance, as indicating the moment when Wordsworth began to suspect the analytic intellect as a source of moral wisdom. The young leader of the band of borderers is generous and high-minded; the tempter Oswald is an elder man and a man of more powerful understanding; by the play of a sceptical intelligence, by sophistries of the understanding, by the promise of spiritual emancipation, he darkens the natural conscience of his victim and leads him into pitiless and irreparable crime. For young Marmaduke nothing more remains in life except a wild and desolate search for expiation.

"Wordsworth," as I have elsewhere written,

"recovered, as a sick man recovers, not through logical processes, but by secret operations of nature, and a gradual recuperative tendency." He turned away from mere speculation; he permitted himself once again to feel. By the healing influences of nature, by the gentle admonitions and quickening sympathies of his sister Dorothy, a communion between his intellect, his affections, and his imagination was re-established. In place of humanitarian dreams came a deep interest in the joys and sorrows of individual men and women; through his interest in these he was led back to a study of the mind of man and those laws which connect the work of the creative imagination with the play of the passions. He had begun again to think nobly of the world and of human life. And at this moment Wordsworth found a friend, who like himself had hoped, like himself had been disappointed, and who now had found a solution for the problems which had vexed him in a conception of the world and of life at once philosophical and religious. In external nature and in the evolution of human society Coleridge recognized a Divine Presence and a Divine process. Such a conception seemed the true interpretation of the phenomena of Wordsworth's own mind; it was confirmed by his highest moods and clearest moments of insight and of rapture. The optimism of Coleridge met the need of Wordsworth's nature. Not through searchings of the analytic intellect had he made his discoveries of truth, but through passionate contemplation and through joy. For him wisdom lived before all else in happiness, which was, indeed, another name for inward harmony, the sane co-operation of all those powers that work for wisdom. Discontent, cynicism, gloom, might be the self-indulgence of less strenuous minds. For his own part he resolved to resist every invasion of sadness as a lethargy of the soul, or to convert sadness to some glorious gain. Joy became to him more than a desire; it became a duty.[1]

What remained to Wordsworth from his early Revolutionary faith? The Revolution spoke of nature, of simplification, of humanity, of new hopes for the race, of reason, of equality, of fraternity (I omit for the present moment the word "liberty"). Wordsworth retained his faith in the beneficence of nature; he sings of the wedding of man's mind "to this goodly universe, in love

[1] What is here said with the utmost brevity will be found stated at large in M. Émile Legouis' admirable study, "La Jeunesse de William Wordsworth."

and holy passion." He does not attempt to deny the facts of evil and of pain. "He can stand," writes one of his critics, "in the shadow of death and pain, ruin and failure, with a sympathy that is almost painful in its quiet intensity; yet the sense 'of something far more deeply interfused' which 'makes our noisy years seem moments in the being of the eternal silence,' the faith in the omnipotence 'of love and man's unconquerable mind,' is never destroyed or even weakened in him. The contemplation of evil and pain always ends with him, by an inevitable recoil, in an inspired expression of his faith in the good which transmutes and transfigures it, as clouds are changed into manifestations of the sunlight they strive to hide." [1] He retained his desire to simplify life, and he proved its genuineness by that "plain living" which preserved him from mean anxieties and degrading shifts, and rendered possible the "high thinking" of a poet's calling. He lost none of his sense of the dignity of man as man; he believed in a high destiny for the human race. He thought less, indeed, than formerly of man in an abstract way and of the rights of man; but he entered far more deeply into the joys and sorrows

[1] Edward Caird, Essays on Literature and Philosophy, vol. i. pp. 188, 189.

of individual men, honoring before all else those
strong, permanent, and universal passions which
are found in the cottage as well as in the palace,
or which, as he believed, may be found with
greater purity and undivided strength in the
cottage. He ceased to speak of fraternity and
equality; but this was because he perceived a
certain effeminacy in levelling down the truth
to general notions and ambitious words, and
ascertained that a truer sense of human fellow-
ship arose from close and sympathetic contact
with his fellows. Still he paid homage to the
"universal heart" of man; still he believed in
one great society on earth of "the noble living
and the noble dead." If he wrote of a Michael
or a Margaret, a Pedler or a Leech-gatherer, it
was without a single touch of condescension or
of patronage; even their manner of speech, he
maintained, includes everything that is needful
and everything that is best for the uses of poetry.
He honored reason in the mastery which man
had obtained over matter, in the scientific advance and mechanical progress of the age. But
he also honored the affections, the imagination,
the moral sense, the spiritual insight of men;
and he feared lest reason, operating apart from
these, should darken the light that is in us, and

lest the rage for wealth stimulated by mechanical inventions should create a new serfdom for the toiler. Who at the close of the nineteenth century will assert that his fears were without a certain warrant?

I reserved that great watchword of the Revolution, — Liberty. There was unquestionably a danger that in his study of the individual man Wordsworth might in some measure have lost his interest in national life and the larger concerns of a people. With Coleridge for a time there was a like danger. When the Swiss Cantons were attacked by the French Republic, he wrote his magnificent ode " France," which originally appeared nnder the title of " The Recantation." And a recantation indeed it is; a poem of disillusion regarding the hopes for society which he had formed in connection with the French Revolution. " The Sensual and the Dark," he cries, " rebel in vain, slaves by their own compulsion." Liberty, as he had conceived it, he now sorrowfully admits, cannot be realized by society, under any form of human government; " it belongs," as Coleridge's argument prefixed to the ode declares, " to the individual man, so far as he is pure, and inflamed with the love and adoration of God in Nature." Such a doctrine approaches

hazardously near to political despair. Southey's
early enthusiasm had also declined; there was a
considerable risk that he might narrow his sympathies to those which concerned his personal
friends and his fireside, or might lose some of his
large-heartedness in the mere accumulation and
rearrangement of knowledge. "How does time
mellow down our opinions," he wrote. ". . . I
have contracted my sphere of action within the
little circle of my own friends, and even my
wishes seldom stray beyond it. . . . I want a little
room to arrange my books in, and some Lares of
my own."   And again: "I have declared war
against metaphysics, and would push my arguments, as William Pitt would his successes, even
to the extermination of the enemy. 'Blessed be
the hour I 'scaped the wrangling crew.'"   There
are symptoms here of the sinking of a flame
into ashes. Southey was indeed well qualified to
sing his "Hymn to the Penates;" but his heart
was also made to extend its generous warmth
beyond his home, and in his imagination there
was something of an epic quality which could
enter into the action of an entire people. Was
moral exhaustion, in the opening years of the
nineteenth century, to follow the excesses of
sentimentalism and the excesses of anarchy?

Was the story to be a sorry story of disillusion for this group of young poets, whose hopes had been so high, whose spirit had been so generous and ardent? Were they to exclaim with Brutus, "Liberty, I worshipped thee, and I find thee but a Shade"? Or were they to be content each with the liberty of the individual man, preserved for each in the citadel of his own soul?

A second springtime of enthusiasm was happily in store for them. The war proclaimed against the French Republic had shocked their moral sense, and caused an inward disruption, the filial love of England still living in their hearts, while indignation against the action of England divided them from their country. But when the Republic was transformed into a military despotism, when it entered upon wars of conquest, when the vast tyranny of one ruler, with his satraps and underlords, was established over Europe, when England stood alone against the world in defence of freedom, in defence of humanity, the public spirit of these young men was again aroused; they found themselves restored to their native land; and hopes and fears, indignation, pride, and patriotism, were fused into one glowing mass. And so a second springtime arrived. A great epic of battle, heroism, agony, death, and victory seemed to evolve itself before men's eyes; more than this, — Englishmen themselves were among the combatants; and all the epic passions were aroused.

"Five years of life," cries De Quincey, "it was worth paying down for the privilege of an outside place on a mail-coach when carrying through the country the news of a victory." "Horses!" he exclaims, in his inspiriting description of the start from Lombard Street, "can these be horses that bound off with the action and gesture of leopards? What stir! — what sea-like ferment! what a thundering of wheels! what a trampling of hoofs! what a sounding of trumpets! what farewell cheers! what redoubling peals of brotherly congratulation, connecting the name of the particular mail — 'Liverpool forever!' — with the name of a particular victory 'Badajos forever!' or 'Salamanca forever!' The half-slumbering consciousness that all night long and all the next day — perhaps for even a longer period — many of these mails, like fire racing along a train of gunpowder, will be kindling at every instant new successions of burning joy, has an obscure effect of multiplying the victory itself, by multiplying to the imagination into infinity the stages of its progressive diffusion. A fiery arrow seems to be let loose, which from that moment is destined to travel, without intermission, westwards for three hundred miles — northwards for six hundred — and the sympathy of our Lombard Street friends at parting is exalted a hundred fold by a sort of visionary sympathy with the yet slumbering sympathies which in so vast a succession we are going to awake."

Such was the temper of the time, and some of its breadth of interests and depth of passion passed into De Quincey's opium-dreams : "' Deeper than ever plummet sounded ' I lay inactive. Then, like a chorus, the passion deepened. Some greater interest was at stake, some mightier cause than ever yet the sword had pleaded, or trumpet had proclaimed. Then came sudden alarms ; hurryings to and fro, trepidations of innumerable fugitives, I knew not whether from the good cause or the bad ; darkness and lights ; tempest and human faces ; and at last, with the sense that all was lost, female forms, and the features that were all the world to me." It is a dream of epic proportions, into which are woven the passions inspired by a great national struggle.

The noblest products in the field of pure literature which the Napoleonic wars have left us are Wordsworth's political sonnets, his poem " The

Happy Warrior," and his pamphlet on the " Convention of Cintra." The sonnets are records of the most impassioned moments in the history of Wordsworth's imagination, as it dealt with public events from 1802 to the battle of Waterloo. Many of them are concerned, like his prose pamphlet, with affairs in Spain. The cumulative force of the great drama that was unrolling itself was not felt until the struggle in the Peninsula had become a central point of interest. Until then the patriotic temper was, as Wordsworth describes it, a temper of fortitude, a " sedate and stern melancholy, which had no sunshine, and was exhilarated only by the lightnings of indignation." But with the rising of the Spanish people there came a mighty change: "We were instantaneously animated, and from that moment the contest assumed the dignity which it is not in the power of anything but hope to bestow; and, if I may dare to transfer language, prompted by a revelation of the state of being that admits not of decay or change, to the concerns and interests of our transitory planet, from that moment 'this corruptible put on incorruption, and this mortal put on immortality.'" Wordsworth has hardly overstated the truth. From the date of the Spanish rising, Napoleon could no longer

stand forth as the representative of democratic
ideas; the principle of nationality was mani-
festly on the side of his adversaries; its influence
was sensible in Germany as well as in the Pyre-
nean Peninsula; the moral force of Europe was
arrayed against the material might of its con-
queror. "This is not a quarrel of governments,"
Coleridge wrote, in his "Letters on the Spaniards,"
published in the "Courier." ". . . If the Peace of
Amiens made the nation unanimous in its dread
of French ambition, it was the noble efforts of
Spanish patriotism that first restored us, without
distinction of party, to our characteristic enthusiasm for *liberty*, and . . . enabled us once more
to utter the names of our Hampdens, Sidneys,
and Russells, without hazard of alarming the quiet
subject, or of offending the zealous loyalist."

Now it was that Wordsworth many a time
would start after midnight from Allan Bank
to the Raise Gap to meet at two o'clock in the
morning the carrier bringing the newspaper from
Keswick. "It would not be easy," he said, "to
conceive with what a depth of feeling I entered
into the struggle carried on by the Spaniards for
their deliverance from the usurped power of the
French." The passion of the time was experienced hardly less deeply by others. On the

declaration of Westminster on the subject of the
Spanish war, Walter Scott wrote to his friend
Ellis: "Tell Mr. Canning that the old women
of Scotland will defend the country with their
distaffs rather than that troops enough be not
sent to make good so noble a pledge." "The
news from Spain," Scott writes, a month later,
"gave me such a mingled feeling, that I never
suffered so much in my whole life from the disorder of spirits occasioned by affecting intelligence. . . . I love a drum and a soldier as heartily
as ever Uncle Toby did; and between the pride
arising from our gallant bearing and the deep
regret that so much bravery should run to waste,
I spent a most disordered and agitated night, never
closing my eyes but what I was harassed with
visions of broken ranks, bleeding soldiers, dying
horses, and 'all the currents of a heady fight.'"
On his journeys never did Scott omit to take
with him the largest map of the seat of war that
he could procure. Upon this, Lockhart tells us,
he was perpetually poring, tracing by means of
black and white pins the movements of the con-
tending forces. When in 1811 a London com-
mittee was formed to collect subscriptions for the
relief of the Portuguese, Scott begged to be permitted to contribute to the fund such profits as

might be gained by a poem written on a subject connected with the patriotic struggle. As soon as leisure could be snatched, he set to work upon his " Vision of Don Roderick," a poem not in his happiest manner; the Gothic vestibule, as Jeffrey put it, being hardly in keeping with the modern structure to which it conducts; yet one which will always remain interesting as an evidence of the deep commotion caused in the writer's spirit by the events in Spain.

"It was a time unparalleled in history," Southey wrote, "and a more glorious one never has and never can be exhibited to the world." Southey's friend, Landor, who had in him something of the paladin of romance, at this moment put his poetry into the form of action. He would equip a troop and lead them into battle on Spanish soil as the first English volunteer. On reaching Corunna he made over ten thousand reals to the governor for the relief of the inhabitants of Venturada, whose houses had been burnt to the ground by the French, and announced that he was ready to pay the expenses of any volunteers to the number of a thousand who were willing to join him: "I shall travel with them on foot, and fight along with them, glorying to serve under the command of any brave Spaniard who has taken up arms in

the defence of religion and liberty." Landor's
wisdom in the conduct of life was not equal to
his chivalry. He quarrelled with the English
envoy; his military feats were no more than
petty skirmishes; he was devoured with impatience for a larger field of action. "What the
alleged affront of the envoy had begun," writes
his biographer, Forster, "the affair of Cintra and
its disasters completed: his troop dispersed or
melted away; and he came back to England in
as great a hurry as he had left it." The ill-considered expedition to the Peninsula at least served
to give local color to Landor's noble dramatic
poem, "Count Julian;" and if things were justly
weighed, perhaps the error of his impetuous outbreak against Stuart might be balanced by the
generous aid he rendered on one occasion to an
exhausted Spanish woman, whose child he carried on his shoulders for six or seven miles.
Quixotry has its follies, but a temper more dis-
creet has not always its ready gallantries.

Coleridge, when contrasting Shakespeare's political wisdom with the high-flying Toryism of
Beaumont and Fletcher and the aristocratic
Whiggism of Massinger, has spoken of our greatest poet as embodying in his historical plays the
permanent politics of human nature. It is a hard

saying to understand or to expound. The permanent politics of human nature, — what are they? Of Wordsworth's "Poems dedicated to National Independence and Liberty" we may assert that if they do not express such "permanent politics," they have assuredly a purport passing beyond the occasions which suggested or inspired them. The passions to which they give utterance, the principles which they announce, are of no less worth and validity for our day than they were for the opening days of the century. They deal not so much with events that pass away as with abiding forces of the heart of man and abiding truths of our corporate life. In external events he seeks an inward moral significance, presses after this, and cannot rest satisfied until he finds it. If we may speak of any single thought as the central thought around which this remarkable group of poems is organized, it is this, — that the true life of a nation resides not in external institutions, not in visible prosperity, not in force of arms, not even in the splendors of individual genius, but in the spiritual energy of the people, in the vitality of that which animates all else, the nation's soul.

In August, 1802, during the short interval of calm which followed the Peace of Amiens, Words-

worth and his sister visited France.   Gazing
westward at evening from the seacoast, he
watched the evening-star as it hung over England,
and his heart turned to the land of his birth with
a fond and tender pride.   Napoleon was elected
First Consul for life at the moment of Wordsworth's arrival at Calais; but there seemed to be
no genuine joy in the event, as far as a foreign
observer could discern, and the prostrate homage
that was paid to power impressed Wordsworth as
something far other than the seemly reverence
which is a gradual growth from roots deep-planted
in the heart.   Great indeed was the alteration of
the public temper since, in the fervid early days
of the Revolution, when the very "senselessness
of joy" was sublime, he had landed with his college companion at the same spot.   August 15th
was Bonaparte's birthday; but Calais was not gay,
nor was the heart of Wordsworth.   He thought
of all the wrongs from which Europe, and more
than Europe, suffered.   He mourned over the
servitude of Venice, the maiden city, mated to the
sea, now dishonored and decayed.   He thought
of the reduction of Saint Domingo, and of the
negro chieftain, Toussaint L'Ouverture, now languishing in some dungeon of France; yet he
sustained a lofty hope that the cause of liberty

had still its untamable auxiliaries in the powers
of nature and in the passions of man, —

> " Thou hast left behind
> Powers that will work for thee: air, earth, and skies;
> There 's not a breathing of the common wind
> That will forget thee; thou hast great allies;
> Thy friends are exultations, agonies,
> And love, and man's unconquerable mind."

On his voyage back to Dover he observed another example of the capricious tyranny of the
ruler of France, — a white-robed negress sat on
deck, one of the afflicted race which had been ex-
pelled by a decree of the government, downcast,
languid, lifeless, except for the tropic fire that still
burned in her eyes.   It was a happiness to tread
the grass of England once again, and to hear the
waves breaking on the chalky shore.   He felt the
mightiness for good of the silver streak of sea;
and yet he knew that the strength and safety of
his country could not lie in this narrow span of
waters; in itself this was nothing; it became a
bulwark of freedom only when brave hearts made
it indeed a barrier flood, — " by the soul only, the
Nations shall be great and free."   And at this
time Wordsworth was not without fears that the
soul of England might be unequal to its trials.
He trembled lest ease and luxury should have
sapped her native hardihood and strength, —

> " Plain living and high thinking are no more ;
> The homely beauty of the good old cause
> Is gone ; our peace, our fearful innocence,
> And pure religion breathing household laws."

At one moment he looked back to the heroic days of the old Republic, and sighed for the return of Milton's spirit, to restore to his countrymen virtue, power, and freedom ; he recalled to mind Vane and Sidney, Harrington and Marvell.   But again he grew ashamed of such unfilial fears ; his feeling towards England was that of a lover or a child ; her glorious past seemed to insure a future no less heroic, —

> " In our halls is hung
> Armory of the invincible knights of old :
> We must be free or die who speak the tongue.
> That Shakespeare spoke ; the faith and morals hold
> That Milton held."

He felt that to hope is a paramount duty laid by Heaven upon the suffering heart of man ; that, while worldlings may tremble for possessions which an accident can cause to wax or wane, the perpetual breath of hope breathes upon every gift of noble origin.   When, in October, 1803, the invasion of England was threatened, although, in presence of the enormous despotism of one man, Wordsworth was almost tempted to a doubt of Providence, against his doubt sprang up a stronger

faith, and with it an indomitable courage. One
thing there is which cannot be forced to yield
before the discipline of the sword, — one thing,
the united soul of a nation.   The poet, rising to
the prophet, dared to anticipate a memorable victory over the invader, and in the sternness of his
enthusiasm could think of the very worst — the
prospect of his brethren slain — with an exultant
joy.

But it was the patriotic struggle in Spain
which called forth Wordsworth's highest ardor.
It seemed to him to be a great outbreak of nature
in the heart of a people on behalf of freedom;
and when in his pamphlet suggested by the Convention of Cintra he weighed "the hopes and
fears of suffering Spain," he felt that the finest
promptings, the truest oracles of political wisdom, came to him in presence of the free powers
of nature, — among the mountain winds or where
the torrents leap down their rocky courses.
From learned Germany, instructed in the lessons
of the schools, less was to be hoped than from
the Iberian peasants.   The pride of intellect and
thought might come to a composition with tyranny ; but the native energy of the soul, embodied
in a few strong instincts and a few plain rules,
was a bulwark for freedom kindred to the moun-

tains and the floods. Wordsworth was not so carried away by his enthusiasm as to be unaware that in all the mechanic part of warfare the advantage lay heavily on the side of the French brigades ; the promise of victory for Portugal and Spain lay in what was invisible, in their moral power, in the righteousness of their cause. "Unbounded," he exclaims, "is the might of martyrdom and fortitude and right," —

> " The power of Armies is a visible thing,
> Formal, and circumscribed in time and space ;
> But who the limits of that power can trace
> Which a brave People into light can bring
> Or hide, at will, — for freedom combating
> By just revenge inflamed?   No foot may chase,
> No eye can follow, to a fatal place
> That power, that spirit, whether on the wing
> Like the strong wind, or sleeping like the wind
> Within its awful caves."

And as Wordsworth in his feeling for external nature found through all its influencings a spiritual Presence communing with his own spirit, so in the sacred passions of a People sacrificing themselves for freedom, for home, for religion, for the hopes of their infants, for the memories of their dead, he seemed to become conscious of an energy not merely human but Divine. It is, indeed, a weakness to seek from miraculous interpositions, from the saints above, or the spells of herb and stone, that virtue which has its residence in the heart of man; but in the instincts of human nature, in hope, in fortitude, in martyrdom, lives and moves the supreme Power of the universe ; through these He builds "the towers of righteousness" as a refuge from the worst disaster ; all that to us seems violent or ghastly form but "links in the chain of His tranquillity." At length the great drama reached its triumphant catastrophe at Waterloo; in January, 1816, a day of general thanksgiving was appointed, and Wordsworth poured forth the solemn hymn which closes his " Poems dedicated to National Independence and Liberty." He ascribes the victory, not to the sword, but to the magnanimity that wielded the sword with irresistible might; and that magnanimity was but a form of His energy who lifteth up and layeth low. And so on the bright January morning, with sunshine sleeping on the snow-clad hills, he sang his song of devout rejoicing, — " Oh, enter now His Temple gate ! "

The pamphlet occasioned by the Convention of Cintra was conceived and written in the spirit of the political sonnets. It forms indeed an undesigned commentary on the poems of the same period. The forces under Junot's command had been defeated by Wellesley at Vimiero. Sir Hew Dalrymple, instead of pressing home the victory, concluded the convention by which the French agreed to evacuate Portugal, and were to be conveyed with their baggage and arms in British ships to France. Wordsworth considers the affair less from a military or a political point of view than from that of a patriotic citizen who studies primarily its moral significance, its effect upon the spirit and temper of the people of the Peninsula. " In the moral qualities," he writes, " and passions which belong to a people must the ultimate salvation of a people be sought for." The national feeling demanded that the defeated French should be compelled to surrender at discretion, or should be exterminated. It was folly to think of supporting the cause of Portugal and Spain by physical strength; while, through a faltering policy, the moral energies of the people were being sapped. The Convention was a compromise of supposed expediency; but in such a case there is one supreme expediency, namely, justice; this alone can satisfy the spirit of an indignant nation : " When wickedness acknowledges no limit but the extent of her power . . . the only worthy or adequate opposition is that of virtue submitting to no circumscription of her endeavors save that of her rights, and aspiring from the impulse of her own ethereal zeal." " It was not," he asserts, " for the soil or for the cities and forts that Portugal was valued, but for the human feeling which was there. . . . We combated for victory in the empire of reason, for strongholds in the imagination." To a certain order of practical statesmen such utterances as these may appear visionary; but it was Napoleon himself, and his calculations were little likely to err on the side of fantastic generosity, who estimated the worth of moral force in warfare as equivalent to three times that of physical force. The lofty enthusiasm which animates Wordsworth's pamphlet cannot be conveyed in a few words; only the reader of its best pages can feel its weight and mass of passion and the inward glow of its argument. What he wrote was, however, ill qualified for producing a popular impression; the sentences move with the sweep of a broad-winged bird, and a pamphlet for immediate effect should pounce, not soar; the mode of dealing with events as moral causes rather than as material effects was suited only to exceptional minds which had some kinship with that of Wordsworth. Delays in publication occurred, and, in the rapid progress of affairs in Spain, when the pamphlet was issued it was already out of date.

A vigorous series of Letters on the Spaniards was contributed by Coleridge to the "Courier;" he would be proud, he said, to consider these as an appendix to Wordsworth's pamphlet. Their spirit is, indeed, in perfect accord with that of his friend's political criticism. The letters aimed at an investigation of the grounds of hope and fear which the history of past ages suggests in the case of war between a people and organized armies, and drew a parallel between the struggle in the Peninsula against the French and that of former times in the Belgic provinces against Philip II. Coleridge's historical study is illuminated and supported by characteristic passages of reflection, and by a constant reference to what he held to be the first principles of political wisdom. Like Wordsworth, he discovers in the energies of the Spanish patriots "a power which mocks the calculations of ordinary statecraft, too subtle to be weighed against mere brute outward force;" a power which he compares to electricity, as infinite in its affinities and infinite in its modes of action; a power which is no other than the insulted free-will of a whole people, steadied by an approving conscience, and reacting against iniquitous compulsion for the common rights of human nature. Against such a power Coleridge argued, like Wordsworth, that the machinery of armies, however perfect that machinery may be, must in the end prove helpless. Those whose fears for Spain were founded on what they termed the facts of the situation forgot the one dominant though invisible fact, — the presence of the spirit which overthrows oppressors. "It is a painful truth," Coleridge writes in a passage which deserves to be remembered, "that those men who appeal most to facts and pretend to take them for their exclusive guide are the very persons who most disregard the light of experience, when it refers them to the mightiness of their own inner nature, in opposition to those forces which they can see with their eyes and reduce to figures upon a slate. And yet, sir, what is history for the greater and more useful part but a voice from the sepulchres of our forefathers, assuring us from their united experience that our spirits are as much stronger than our bodies as they are nobler and more permanent. The historic Muse appears in her loftiest character as the nurse of Hope." In the first war of the French Republic against her foreign invaders, it was faith in ideas which enabled the raw levies to oppose themselves successfully to disciplined battalions. Now, this faith in the invisible rendered the often defeated Spaniards finally invincible. The armies of Napoleon's marshals were a formidable machine of war; but viewed inwardly, they lacked unity and cohesion, they represented only a mass of conflicting self-interests. The better spirit of the Revolution was fighting against them; and Wordsworth and Coleridge felt that in their loyalty to the Spanish cause they retained that which was most precious in the enthusiasm of their earlier days.

The historic Muse, though the "Letters on the Spaniards" invoke her aid, had less close and less frequent communings with Coleridge than with his brother poet, Southey. There was something epical in Southey's imagination. He cared less for ideas than for heroic character and action. His fancy was exhilarated by adventure. He loved to follow the march of great events. In the earlier years of the Napoleonic struggle, while France achieved her unparalleled conquests on land, England held her destined position as mistress of the seas. Her supremacy as a naval power was largely due to the incom-

parable genius for battle and the high self-devo-
tion of Nelson. In his poem of 1806, the
"Character of the Happy Warrior," Wordsworth,
deriving something from the memory of his
brother John, who had gone down with his
vessel in the preceding year, connects with this
his conception of the character of Nelson, and
presents his ideal of the armed champion of his
country. In the mild concerns of ordinary life
he shows himself gracious rather than great.
But this gentle hero of days of tranquillity is
transfigured in the hour of danger. The happy
warrior is one who,

> " if he be called upon to face
> Some awful moment to which Heaven has joined
> Great issues, good or bad, for human kind,
> Is happy as a lover ; and attired
> With sudden brightness, like a man inspired ;
> And through the heat of conflict keeps the law
> In calmness made, and sees what he foresaw."

Southey's " Life of Nelson " may be described
as a miniature prose epic ; it is a simple narrative of heroic action, unencumbered with reflections or lyrical outbreaks of feeling. The book
was designed as a manual for young sailors, to
be carried about by them, until they had treas-
ured in their memory and heart the example of
the chivalric hero, with his high sense of duty,

his patriotism, his humanity. "The best eulogy of Nelson," wrote Southey, "is the faithful history of his actions; the best history, that which shall relate them most perspicuously." His method is that of plain narrative; he made himself master of such material as was then accessible; he disposed of it with admirable skill; and he allowed it to speak for itself. His ardent feelings are held in reserve; but it is they that give his story its steadfast power of wing. Only at the close, and then as if inevitably, comes an outbreak, not of sorrow, but of just pride and exultation: "He cannot be said to have fallen prematurely whose work was done; nor ought he to be lamented, who died full of honors, and at the height of human fame. The most triumphant death is that of the martyr; the most awful, that of the martyred patriot; the most splendid, that of the hero in the hour of victory: and if the chariot and the horses of fire had been vouchsafed for Nelson's translation, he could scarcely have departed in a brighter blaze of glory. He has left us, not indeed his mantle of inspiration, but a name and an example, which are at this hour inspiring hundreds of the youth of England, — a name which is our pride, and an example which will

continue to be our shield and our strength."
To find a parallel for words of such lofty cheer,
we have to turn to those of deeper and more
moving import in which Milton's Manoa sums
up the meaning of the death of the Israelitish
champion.

In his "History of the Peninsular War,"
Southey's method is the same, — that of objec-
tive narrative. It tells an epic story, illustrious
with heroic incident and character. From the
commencement of the contest, Southey had en-
tertained the hope and intention of recording its
events; but he delayed in order to become possessed of the gradually accumulating material.
The hero of the epic is Wellington, and the title
to fame awarded to him by the historian is not
merely that he broke the spell of Napoleon's
supposed omnipotence, not that he defeated the
armies of France, not that his foresight and
enterprise were equalled by his military discretion, not that as a commander he never gave an
opportunity and never lost one, but that by his
achievements he delivered two grievously oppressed nations; secured the safety, honor, and
welfare of England; preserved the general interests of Europe and of the civilized world, and
accomplished his task in the spirit of beneficent

humanity. The eulogy proceeds in words which express the feeling of the time, and which our colder judgment may value at least as a document illustrating its exultant temper.

Many of the persons and incidents of the Peninsular campaigns were commemorated by Southey in a series of " Inscriptions." According to a Welsh triad, the " three utilities " of poetry are " the praise of virtue and goodness, the memory of things remarkable, and to invigorate the affections." To these ends Southey's " Inscriptions " are dedicated, and in this monumental form of verse, for which he found his model in Chiabrera, he became a master. His too fluent style was restrained by the imposed limitation; his feelings were concentrated, and their expression was invigorated by restraint. Readers of the present day, when Southey's verse is little known and, weighted by its masses of heavy mediocrity, has sunk below its deserts, may account for Landor's admiration by the enthusiasm of his friendship; and doubtless some of his unbounded praise is to be ascribed to that cause. But the rare union of marmoreal strength and impulsive feeling which characterizes the best poetry of Landor may be found in one or two of these short pieces by Southey.

That which commemorates the gallant death of Thomas, ensign of the Buffs, has the excellence of exact adequacy; it confers perpetuity on a moment of heroic passion; it precisely hits the mark.

From his early manhood, Southey had been brought into closer relations with Portugal and Spain, with the manners, life, and literature of those countries, than any Englishman of letters of his generation. Wordsworth had been more deeply influenced by France than either of his friends; Coleridge, through his philosophic studies, had been the intimate of Germany; it was to the Spanish Peninsula that Southey's heart turned, if ever it left his native land. The recollection of Cintra was present to him as a living joy; he toiled among the chroniclers and the romancers with a love that made his labors pleasures. The combined action, therefore, of England and Spain in a great patriotic effort aroused his deepest sympathies. Some of the feeling called forth by the war against the French enters into his " Roderick." When the young champion Pelayo takes the vow of devotion to his country and of sacred vengeance against her oppressors, the poet did not think only of the Moorish invaders. The scene is an impressive one, under the blue firmament among the Sierras of Spain. The disguised Roderick, whose crime of passion had led to the entrance of the infidel horde, administers in his religious garb the vow; in presence of the ancient mountains, his native streams, and earth and sky, the noble youth, on whom rest the hopes of his people, swears for himself and his children's children, never to cease from hereditary holy war until the last invader be exterminated or driven from the sacred soil, —

> "Silently
> The people knelt, and when they rose, such awe
> Held them in silence, that the eagle's cry,
> Who far above them, at her highest flight
> A speck scarce visible, gyred round and round,
> Was heard distinctly; and the mountain stream,
> Which from the distant glen sent forth its sounds
> Wafted upon the wind, grew audible
> In that deep hush of feeling, like the voice
> Of waters in the stillness of the night."

"The Curse of Kehama" by its subject is remote from European interests; we are encircled by monstrous gods of Hindoo mythology; but even here the passions of the time effect an entrance. The poem, begun at Lisbon in 1801, was finished at Keswick in November, 1809. The almighty Rajah, as the narrative proceeded, identified himself in Southey's imagination with the ruler of Europe. Kehama, most implacable of tyrants, by unholy prayers and sacrifices, has made himself a rival to the supreme deities themselves; he aspires to drink the cup of immortality, and to assume the throne of Padalon. But Seeva, the god of righteous vengeance, is still unconquered; he opens upon the profane tyrant his eye of anger; the wrath-beam falls; and the Rajah, made immortal for punishment, not for triumph, moves under the decree of divine power, not to fill the throne, but to stand forever as one of its tortured supporters. "O fool!" exclaims the poet, and his words were addressed in idea to the Napoleon-Kehama of Europe, —

> "O fool of drunken hope and frantic vice!
>   Madman! to seek for power beyond thy scope
>   Of knowledge, and to deem
>   Less than Omniscience could suffice
>   To wield Omnipotence!"

The conclusion of the poem was Southey's protest against an error, which of all others, as Coleridge declared in the "Courier," was the special danger of the time, — the "inward prostration of the soul before enormous power, and a readiness to palliate and forget all iniquities to which prosperity had wedded itself."

But Southey's most impassioned pleading against Bonaparte is to be found in his "Ode written during the Negotiations for Peace in 1814," a poem of which the author of "Philip van Artevelde" asserted that since Milton's great sonnet on the massacre in Piedmont there has been no occasional poem equal to it in grandeur and power; "nor any," he adds, "equal to it in art." It has certainly the distinction of being the fiercest lyrical invective in our language; and the invective is of a lofty kind, inspired by public passion, by sacred indignation, by a deep loyalty to the human hopes and natural charities which had been violated, by a sense of the great human fraternity of the noble living and the noble dead, by an ear open to the invocation of the spirits of just men to the everlasting Judge of righteousness. "How long, O Lord! Holy and Just, how long!"

The ideas of liberty and of the fraternity of nations had been lost by France during the Napoleonic wars. The idea of social equality remained. Southey was too much swayed by passion to recognize or interpret the complete significance of the great events of his age. He failed to perceive the beneficent part of that work which Napoleon terribly accomplished.

His deep interest in social reforms saved Southey
from becoming obstructive or stationary; but his
political creed ceased to have in it the elements
of progress. The passions which he had endured
were exhausting and now craved repose. He did
not in the years that followed alter the position
which he had taken up. Coleridge continued
his task of renovating old ideas. Wordsworth
travelled onward to the heights of old age,
illuminated by a tranquil evening light.[1]

---

[1] Southey's political ideas are versified in the Second Part
of "The Poet's Pilgrimage to Waterloo;" the First Part,
describing his journey to the scene of war, is picturesque and
sometimes impassioned; the allegory which follows concerning
the false wisdom of the age and the true hopes of man, cannot
be said to attain more than respectable mediocrity. Unfortunately, the author imagined that he was a philosophical poet.

It is somewhat surprising that Scott should have failed in
the battle poetry of his "Field of Waterloo." The war-lyrics
of the time which survive are few. Wolfe's "Burial of Sir
John Moore" was founded on a passage in Southey's contribution to the "Edinburgh Annual Register," 1808. Campbell,
an ardent sympathizer with the French Revolution, had himself
seen something of continental war in 1800. "Since the arrival
of the gallant Republicans," he writes from Ratisbon, "we have
many specimens of military evolutions extremely striking.
Such fiery countenances and rapid manœuvres as these active
little fellows exhibit are only to be expected from the conquerors of Lodi and Marengo. It would raise every spark
of enthusiasm in your heart to see them marching with stately
and measured steps to the war-song of Liberty." The stanzas
of the "Battle of the Baltic" are happily described by one of
Campbell's critics as "salvoes of artillery."

VI

RENEWED REVOLUTIONARY ADVANCE:
MOORE, LANDOR, BYRON, SHELLEY

RENEWED REVOLUTIONARY ADVANCE

IN one of Moore's "Fables for the Holy Alliance," he describes a dream which is meant for an allegory of the European politics of the time. A palace of ice rises before him in his dream like that which the Empress Anne built in 1740, and, like the Empress's palace, situated on the Neva. In this icy structure the Emperor Alexander is giving a ball, to entertain the monarchs and ambassadors of the Holy Alliance. The gathering is stately, but sensible of the chill, — "shivering in grand illumination." The Czar waltzes briskly; for has not Madame Krudener assured him that there is no danger, and that the frost will last forever? Suddenly, however, the massy walls of the palace are seized with an ill-omened dripping; the floors grow slippery beneath the royal feet. A fandango is loudly called for; but scarcely has the whirl begun, scarcely has the strain been heard, than an angry beam of morning sunlight flames through the chambers, and the cry goes up, " A thaw! a thaw!" Why, asks the dreamer, will monarchs caper thus in palaces without foundation? Instantly everything is in a flow, — crowns, sceptres, fiddles, decorations; the royal arms carved in ice begin to dissolve; the double-headed eagles let the globes slip from their claws; poor old Louis' *fleurs-de-lys* are surely water-lilies. But worse follows, — the kings and kaisers themselves are in a melting mood; just as the Czar is about to issue a sublime ukase forbidding the admission of light, he streams and sinks; Louis, like the sugar-king of a Twelfth-night cake in some urchin's mouth, melts into a shapeless mass. In a minute all is gone, the glittering dome of ice and those beneath it, — kings, fiddlers, emperors. Only one thing is seen and heard, — the bright river rushing forward,

> " Happy as an enfranchis'd bird,
> And prouder of that natural ray,
> Shining along its chainless way, —
> More proudly happy thus to glide
>   In simple grandeur to the sea,
> Than when, in sparkling fetters tied,
> 'T was deck'd with all that kingly pride
>   Could bring to light its slavery!"

Madame Krudener, the she-prophet, may make what she pleases of the dream; it is not the dreamer's part to attempt an interpretation.

Wordsworth and Southey had exulted over the fall of Napoleon, and hailed the return of freedom to Europe.   A despot had indeed been overthrown; an overwhelming danger had been averted; but the battle of Waterloo did not bring liberty to the nations of the Continent.   A month after Napoleon had sailed for his island of exile and imprisonment, the Emperors of Russia and Austria, with King Frederick William, signed the treaty on which the peace of Europe was to rest. Lord Castlereagh, a little later, agreed on behalf of England to an alliance which should secure the future tranquillity of the emancipated peoples. The alliance of September, 1815, was "Holy," because the contracting monarchs declared that both in the administration of their respective states and in their political relations with every other government they would " take for their sole guide the precepts of the holy religion of our Saviour, — namely, the precepts of justice, Christian charity, and peace."   There followed immediately the proscriptions and court-martials of the Bourbon restoration.   Marshal Ney was shot in the gardens of the Luxembourg Palace.   Murat, the exking of Naples, was shot in front of the castle of Pizzo.   The White Terror spread over the south of France.   The so-called Law of Amnesty in

January, 1816, drove into exile many of those who had been conspicuous in war, in statecraft, and in art. Liberty of the press was suspended, and personal liberty lay at the mercy of an ultra-royalist majority. In Spain the Inquisition was re-established, and hundreds of Spanish patriots were put to death. The map of Europe was re-formed with an entire disregard to the principle of nationality. Old free cities and old republics disappeared. The Austrian ruled in Venice. Belgium and Holland, notwithstanding the differences of language, religion, and popular feeling, were united under one king. Norway was forced into subjection to the crown of Sweden. A population of two and a half millions was severed from France. England, indeed, showed a rare moderation as regards territorial aggrandizement, but she showed entire unconcern for popular liberties, for the security of which she had pledged herself. A few statesmen sitting in congress disposed at their pleasure of the loyalty of millions of European citizens. Moore was hardly extravagant when he spoke of the royal saints dipping the sponge in holy water to wipe out all human rights. Benbow was the name of a publisher who brought out infamous and irreligious books. " I can't help thinking," cries Moore,

> " (though to kings
> I must, of course, like other men bow),
> That when a Christian monarch brings
> Religion's name to gloss such things —
> Such blasphemy out-Benbows Benbow."

And again he has a parable for the occasion, — that of a friar and a king who change their cloaks, and who, each in his new disguise, behaves so vilely that Religion has to be packed off to the madhouse, while Royalty is dismissed to Bridewell. The hopes of Wordsworth and Southey after the battle of Waterloo were not fulfilled ; indeed, they might seem almost as delusive as the extravagant dreams which had flattered them in the opening days of the French Revolution.

The problem which lay before Europe was how to unite order with freedom ; in the reaction the monarchs and their representatives thought of order first, and of freedom little, if at all. But the people still thought of freedom ; they could not forget the lessons, for good and for evil, of the Revolution, nor the recent lessons of the Napoleonic wars, which had so strongly called forth throughout Germany and Spain the sentiment of nationality. A series of Revolutionary movements was the result. In 1820 insurrectionary disturbance broke out in Spain and in Italy. Ferdinand found himself compelled to accept a liberal constitution. Convents were suppressed; the Jesuits were banished; the Inquisition was overthrown. The Carbonari promoted an insurrection at Naples; there was revolt in Sicily; there was revolution in Portugal; in Wallachia and Moldavia the people rose; the Greek patriotic flame was lit. In England the Reform movement gathered strength; in Ireland a cry went up for Catholic emancipation. The order attained by the politicians of Vienna and the crowned heads of the Holy Alliance was not a stable order. The thaw of Moore's fable had begun, and the palace of ice was visibly dripping.

The time was one of dissonance. The chief literary exponents in England of the Revolutionary spirit in its earlier days had gone over to the party of order. Wordsworth pleaded with the freeholders of Westmoreland against the acceptance of such an agitator as Brougham for the representation of the county; or he occupied himself in tracing in a series of sonnets the history of the English Church. Southey, while advocating not a few wise reforms, engaged vigorously as a Quarterly Reviewer in defending the established order of things. Coleridge's influence was a liberalizing influence upon thought; but it rather interpreted existing institutions and ideas into new and deeper meanings than aimed at any reorganization of the social and political framework. In the other camp Cobbett uttered vigorous denunciations of taxation, rotten boroughs, fund-holders, and stock-jobbers; but Cobbett's Radicalism, as Fitzjames Stephen has remarked, had in it a curious and almost a romantic strain of conservatism. Hazlitt unpacked his heart with words; lavished abuse on the renegades who had deserted the objects of their early devotion; lashed out at friend and foe; sighed for the happiness of the days before the great Emperor's fall, and reconstructed in his imagination the Napoleonic legend. But Hazlitt's arguments were little more than the props of his passions. Leigh Hunt had a certain bright chivalry on behalf of whatever assumed to itself the cherished name or the aspect of Liberty; at times he could present a gallant front to her foes. But Hunt's shafts, if occasionally keen, were always light-timbered, and rather annoyed the enemy than achieved their ruin. He was framed less for the rough tumble of English radical politics than for "dance and Provençal song and sun-burnt mirth." At this time truth and justice were painfully divided between the party of order and the party of progress. There was no thinker,

no man of action, who could bring together and
co-ordinate the several fragments of truth. It
was at home and abroad a period of much moral
confusion. For many serious minds the ideas of
the Revolution were discredited by the anarchy
to which they had led, and by the military despotism which had taken that anarchy into itself and
enlarged its borders. For many young and passionate hearts the ideas of the party of order were
discredited by the new tyrannies, the cant of religion, the sale of peoples, the reckless indifference
to the hopes and desires of the multitude. It
was hard at such a time to find a faith, and the
danger was great that a mere assertion of egoism
and self-will might take the place of a faith.

In Continental politics the bounding lines between right and wrong were perhaps clearer than
in the politics of England, where the old institutions of the country had borne a great strain well,
and the demand for change could be met by for-
cible arguments for conservation. Certainly, for
an Englishman exiled from his native land, the
traditions of the heart were fewer and less em-
barrassing; he would naturally be caught into
the European movement, and cease to view things
from an insular standpoint. There was, however,
one portion of the United Kingdom where the

traditions favored, not conservation, but change. The memory of confiscations, of ruined trade, of religious disabilities, of outraged sentiment, still lived in Ireland; but Ireland possesses, or once possessed, a happy art of mingling smiles with tears and laughter with indignation. It was in the early days of the Bourbon restoration that the interesting family of Mr. Phil Fudge visited Paris. Old letters of travel are not always entertaining, but those edited by " Thomas Brown the younger" in 1818 deserve to be remembered, and perhaps some persons will think that Fadladeen, Mokanna, Lalla Rookh, and a sentimental Peri are hardly as good company as Mr. Philip, his hopeful son Bob, the patriotic Mr. Phelim Connor, and that romantic Irish maiden, Miss Biddy, who communicates her tender passions and her experiences of foreign travel so naïvely to her correspondent of Clonakilty in Ireland. The head of the house was one of those gentlemen whose secret services in Ireland, under the mild ministry of Lord Castlereagh, had been gratefully remunerated, and, like his friend and associate, Thomas Reynolds the informer, he had retired upon the reward of his honest industry; but still he is ready to report such information as he may acquire to his revered patron. On

Lord Castlereagh's suggestion, Mr. Fudge has undertaken to write an account of his travels in France, a good orthodox work of the kind that was greatly needed, —

> "To expound to the world the new — thingummie — science"

(it is Miss Biddy who describes the purport of the book, and her views on politics are somewhat vague), —

> "Found out by the — what's its name? — Holy Alliance,
> And prove to mankind that their rights are but folly,
> Their freedom a joke (which it *is*, you know, Dolly).
> 'There's none,' said his Lordship, 'if *I* may be judge,
> Half so fit for this great undertaking as Fudge!'"

He is accompanied by that gilded youth, Bob, who has come to study — at least the culinary art of Paris; no longer the sheepish Bob of rural Ireland, —

> "Lord! he's quite altered, they've made him a dandy;
> A thing, you know, whisker'd, great-coated, and lac'd,
> Like an hour-glass, exceedingly small in the waist."

Miss Biddy has gowns no less amazing than Bob's great-coat, and a bonnet

> "so beautiful! high up, and poking,
> Like things that are put to keep chimneys from smoking."

She has a lively sense of existence; enjoys the twinkling feet of Fanny Bias in Flora, and the dark dishevelled hair of the Biggotini as Psyche, with those pious plays — quite charming and very religious — given at the theatre of St. Martin. The fourth of the party is an earnest youth, Phelim Connor, a third cousin, poor but handsome, with the Napoleonic nose and chin, who for charity's sake has been nominated tutor to the curled darling Mr. Bob. Phelim is Irish and Catholic to the backbone ; a dark and determined enemy to all oppressors ; and one who can exhale his wrath in eloquent words. By the happy choice of persons for his little epistolary drama, Moore was enabled to express his Irish gayety, his Irish satirical vein, his Irish political passions and aspirations. Mr. Fudge the elder's book, by and by to be published, will prove

> " that all the world, at present,
> Is in a state extremely pleasant ;
> That Europe — thanks to royal swords
> And bay'nets, and the Duke's commanding,
> Enjoys a peace — which, like the Lord's,
> Passeth all human understanding."

And at the same moment when he makes his pleasing report to Lord Castlereagh, poor Phelim Connor is relieving his overburdened soul in vengeful words, many of which — for he is an intemperate young man — have to be represented by asterisks. Never can he return to Ireland

while the withering hand of bigot power lies
heavy on his country; nay, wheresoever he flies
the scourge pursues him, —

> "Turn where he will the wretched wand'rer views,
> In the bright, broken hopes of all his race,
> Countless reflections of the Oppressor's face.
> Everywhere gallant hearts, and spirits true,
> Are serv'd up victims to the vile and few;
> While E—gl—d everywhere — the general foe
> Of Truth and Freedom, wheresoe'er they glow —
> Is first, when tyrants strike, to aid the blow.
>
> .   .   .   .
>
> Worthy associate of that band of kings,
> That royal rav'ning flock, whose vampire wings
> O'er sleeping Europe treacherously brood,
> And fan her into dreams of promis'd good,
> Of hope, of freedom — but to drain her blood!"

Through his young Irish patriot Moore expresses his own detestation of "the grand con-
spiracy of kings," who had bartered and weighed,
as so much dust, the world of thinking souls.
He describes the joy that filled Europe at the
downfall of Napoleon; the long sigh of the peoples for justice, liberty, repose; and then he
breaks forth against the Royal slave-mart, the
broken charters, the rapine of aristocrats, the
servitude of the press, the mockery of reason
in high places. Napoleon was perfidious, crimi-

nal, a trampler on human freedom; but at least
he had a genius formed

> "for nobler things
> Than lie within the grasp of *vulgar* kings."

Whereupon Moore, in his happy way, saves
himself from the accusation of overloaded rhetoric, and lightens the spirit of his readers, by a
return to Gatti's rose-water and the delectable
ices at Tortoni's.

We care too well for Miss Biddy Fudge to
follow her to the days of her decline, when she
was Protestant and Tory, when Exeter Hall took
the place of Tortoni's, and the flirt had retro-
graded to the saint.   Moore, in his own manner
of satire, gay yet bitter, was happier than when
he occupied himself in spreading the stage-gauze
of his Oriental scenes, or performed the feat, as
Hazlitt describes it, of converting the wild harp
of Erin into a musical snuff-box.   But there are
higher forms of literature than the letters of the
Fudge family.   Among the English literary opponents of the Reaction the most illustrious
names are three,— those of Landor, Byron, and
Shelley.   Landor's position in politics has been
accurately defined by his biographer, Mr. Sidney
Colvin.   He stood midway between the party of
conservation and the party of revolt.   He was

not a democrat; his sympathies were, indeed, alive to the joys and sorrows of the people; but he was essentially an aristocrat of the intellect. His admiration for the majesty of individual character was unbounded; and he held that a "mob" was not "worth a man." His ideal of government resembled that of Milton, a republic ruled by an oligarchy of virtue and of wisdom. The philosophical dogmas of the Revolution had no interest for one who regarded abstract speculation with a lofty scorn. His indignation against the new despotisms of Europe was deep; but in English politics, while he desired, like his friend Southey, to correct many things, he would change little. "His chief practical exhortations," writes Mr. Colvin, "were against wars of conquest and annexation; against alliance with the despotic powers for the suppression of insurgent nationalities; against the over-endowment of ecclesiastical dignitaries; in favor of the removal of Catholic disabilities; in favor of factory acts, of the mitigation of the penal laws, and of ecclesiastical and agrarian laws for the relief of the Irish." Three Italian orations of Landor against the Holy Alliance seem to have been rewritten in English, and were sent for publication to London; unhappily, no trace of

these has been recovered. Their general spirit
may be inferred from certain of the "Imaginary
Conversations;" we cannot doubt that they were
impetuous pleas against tyranny, or that their
impetuosity was moulded into stateliness of form.

The first volume of the "Imaginary Conversations" (1824) was dedicated to Major-General
Stopford, adjutant-general in the army of Co-
lombia. Landor was deeply interested in the
success of the South American republics,— partly,
he says, because he wished every nation under
heaven to be independent; partly, because he
thought it would be advantageous to England
that some counterpoise against the power of the
United States should be found on the American
continent. Mourning over the feebleness of public spirit in his own country and the rarity of
political abilities, he chose to place his noble
volume of prose in the hands of an Englishman,
who seemed to him to have risen above the self-
ishness and frivolity of the time, and who had
aided one of the republics which sprang into
existence at the voice of Bolivar. The second
volume is inscribed to General Mina, the famous
chief of the Spanish guerillas; and with Mina
the writer pleads on behalf of the young republics of the West. He desired to see in South

17

America, not a loose and turbulent democracy, but a confederacy against external tyranny, against dependence and usurpation, against "institutions not founded upon that equable, sound, beneficent system, to which the best energies of man, the sterner virtues, the milder charities, the comforts and satisfactions of life, its regulated and right affections, the useful arts, the ennobling sciences, with whatever is innocent in glory or useful in pleasure, owe their origin, their protection, their progress, and their maturity." Landor's scorn for what may be called the metaphysics of Revolution preserved him from the vacuous rhetoric and the bandying of popular catchwords which are dear to the heart of some prophets of democracy. He was in no sense of the school of the prophets. His conception of a free, adult, proud, and cultivated nation has a grandeur derived from the definite and positive character of his imagination. In his private life Landor was the prey of sudden and violent passions; all the more remarkable are the sanity and virile strength of his political convictions. Their tendency is essentially constructive; if he loved liberty like Milton, he loved it, like Milton also, because he perceived that it is the condition of noble vigor. No loftier word on the evil influence of despotism in dwarfing the passions and the deeds of men has been spoken than that of Landor's poem which in some editions brings his " Hellenics " to a close, —

> " We are what suns and winds and waters make us;
> The mountains are our sponsors, and the rills
> Fashion and win their nurseling with their smiles.
> But where the land is dim with tyranny,
> There tiny pleasures occupy the place
> Of glories and of duties; as the feet
> Of fabled faeries when the sun goes down
> Trip o'er the grass where wrestlers strove by day."

The heroic ideals of Landor's imagination, derived in part from communion with the great natural aristocrats of all time, helped to save his verse and his prose from the violence and egoism which often confused his life, and which often cleared away as suddenly, like clouds before the wind and sun. He toiled indeed at his art with an intemperate rage that exhausted him; but it was to produce a form of marmoreal purity and permanence, to discover the laws and the lines of ideal majesty or ideal grace.

With Byron it was otherwise: he not only lived in an age of dissonance; there was dissonance in his own nature which helped to make him a representative of the age. The old world of feudal reverences and chivalries was out of date; the new world was not yet born. Byron could not satisfy his hunger for life with abstract doctrines; he could not subsist on ideal hopes and faith; he had a great capacity for pleasure, a strong turn for reality, a certain coarseness of fibre; he devoured whatever the world offered him of enjoyment, both vulgar and lofty, and he found it unsatisfying. No organized body of belief guided his intellect; no system of social duties controlled his heart. Society after the Revolution and during the Reaction lay around him in seeming chaos; what was old had lost authority; what was new had not fully justified itself. At least one thing remained, — the individual will, and the power of that will to rise in revolt and scorn against the surrounding society. And so his poetry is an assertion of the supremacy of the individual will; it is the poetry of revolt; it expresses at least the negative side of the Revolution with unequalled force. It is a cry for freedom, — freedom from the tottering tyrannies of the time, from the tottering creeds, from discredited traditions, from the hypocrisies of vulgar respectability, from cant and sham. But if you were to ask Byron, "How, when freedom has been won, is freedom to be used?" he would have no answer to give. The mere deploy-

ing of the passions and the will flatters his imagination with a sense of power; he considers
little, if at all, the true ends for which the will
should put forth its energies.

To acquire a right feeling for Byron and his
poetry is a discipline in equity. It is easy to
yield to a sense of his power, to the force and
sweep of his genius; it is easy to be repelled by
his superficial insincerity, his license, his cynicism, his poverty of thought, his looseness of
construction, his carelessness in execution. To
know aright the evil and the good is difficult.
It is difficult to feel justly towards this dethroned
idol (presently, perhaps, to be re-enthroned), an
idol in whose composition iron and clay are
mingled with fine gold.

But what interests us in Byron and in Byron's
work is precisely this mingling of noble and
ignoble, of gold and a base alloy. We do not
thank any one for extracting the gold and presenting it alone. We can get swifter and clearer
lyric poetry from Shelley, a truer and finer feeling for nature from Wordsworth, more exquisite
satiric art from Pope, dramatic power incompar-
ably wider and deeper from Shakespeare. Seen
in elegant extracts, Byron is impoverished, or
rather Byron ceases to be Byron. Matthew

Arnold's volume of selections from Byron, compiled with such excellent intentions, proves at least that his poetry is not of the kind that can be pinned in a specimen case, like preserved butterflies. Line upon line, here a little and there a little, is the way in which such work as his should *not* be read. We must take him or leave him as he is, — the immortal spoilt by his age, great and petty, weak and strong, exalted and debased. A glorious wave that curls upon the sea-beach, though it leave sea-wrack and refuse on the sands, is more stimulating, more health-giving, than a pitcher of such salt water in one's dressing-room, even if it be free from every floating weed.

In its mingled elements Byron's poetry represents at once the mind and character of the writer and the temper of his age. He was an aristocrat, and at the same time he was revolutionary. He had the pride of ancestry, but nothing of the hereditary dignity, the fine traditions of civility, the trained mastery of men and events, which belong to the best types of his class. The Revolution and the Reaction helped to spoil him as an English nobleman. In a time of disorder and disintegration he fell into the coarse ways of the *jeunesse dorée* of the period of the Regency. The

taint of vulgar aristocracy helped to spoil him as
a Republican.   He had a strong feeling for the
Revolutionary movement as a destructive force ;
he sympathized with its negative tendencies ; he
enjoyed the sense of emancipation from the old
restraints ; he loved to demonstrate the boundless
freedom of the individual, in his passions, his self-
will, his audacities of belief or unbelief, his scorn
for things commonly regarded with veneration or
esteem.   But he cared little for the principles or
tendencies of the Revolution which are positive,
constructive, social ; he had neither the power of
thought nor the patience which are needed by
one who would build up ; it was enough for him
if he could deliver a reeling blow at despotisms,
half-realized creeds, lifeless conventions, and dull
respectabilities, or could mock at them in their
state of infirmity.   He had lost faith in what
was old, and had not gained a new faith.   He
could do little more than plead for an emancipation of egoism, and into his egoism ran that
sentiment of the infinite, that limitless desire,
which Rousseau's passionate heart, his ardent
feeling for nature, and those boundless horizons
opened by the Revolution had made a common
possession of the time.   He asserted with emphasis the prerogative of man to do what he

likes, where he likes, when he likes, how he likes ; and the privilege of woman to lay her passion at the feet of such a proud insurgent. He idealized in his poetry all revolters against the social order, a Cain, a Corsair, a Manfred, all who seek for isolation, for solitude, or find the end of their being in abandonment to personal passion in disregard of social duty. His mockery was a dissolvent of accepted conventions and traditional manners and morals. He took part in popular movements of political emancipation less in the spirit of faith and hope than because his imagination had been captivated by the new force of the people, because it pleased him to deploy his own energy, and because he hated and despised the spent forces, or what seemed to be such, on the side of conservation. To the last he was haunted by the ghosts of traditional beliefs, which had ceased to live within him as vital powers. He was a democrat among aristocrats and an aristocrat among democrats ; a sceptic among believers and a believer among sceptics. And yet his line of advance was not a *via media*, nor was it determined by a spirit of moderation or critical balance. He never attempted to effect a conciliation between the powers that clashed or jarred within him. A certain intellectual good sense indeed he had, but this was liable to be overpowered by the turbulent rush of his temper; and when a reasonable mood re-emerged, good sense would take the form of ironical laughter at himself and at the world. To his quick sense of humor more than to anything else he owed the sanity which controls or modifies his perturbations of mind. With a keen perception of human folly, he could mock absurdity, affectation, extravagance in other men; it was his merit that he could turn the light of laughter upon himself, and chasten his own follies by ridicule.

He passed in his earliest writings at once from song to satire. In the title of his boyish volume, " Hours of Idleness," there is a touch of an affectation which clung to him in after life ; the verses are the recreation of a gentleman, not the work of a professional scribbler. Let others, like Southey, toil for their daily bread by authorship ; he, for his part, would condescend to letters only as a dilettante. It is characteristic of Byron's two-fold nature that his first appearance should be as a lyrical poet, his second as a satirist; but even in his satire there is a large personal element, — its mockery is not all righteous indignation, but the recoil of pride and resentment. As a lyrical

poet he was always fortunate or unfortunate as it
were by force of circumstances.   He did not
weave his lyric out of an impersonal theme made
his own by occult processes of the imagination.
He had little of the shaping power of imagination which is seen in an eminent degree in the
best lyrics of Keats.   He needed the impact of
events, — public events or events in his individual life.   If he wrote with an insufficient impulse from without, the product was often a base
kind of rhetoric, of which we may find frequent
examples in his shorter pieces, or in the shapeless and sometimes tawdry lyrical passages of
"Heaven and Earth."   If he was struck hard by
events, — events in the material or the ideal
sphere, — there came a resonant response; his
strangely discordant powers were for the moment
fused, and he uttered his feelings with incomparable energy and directness.   Pride and passion,
love and hatred, grief and joy, flowed together
and flowed forth in one strong, abounding
stream.

In his "English Bards and Scotch Reviewers"
Byron showed small literary sagacity, but he
struck with force, and proved that he was virile as
a combatant.   The blow, he said, "knocked me
down, but I got up again.   The effect upon me

was rage and resistance." He uses the metre of
Pope, but in Byron's hands it became more of a
cutlass than a stiletto. He lays about him with
little discrimination among the poets of the new
Romantic and Naturalistic schools, — Scott, Coleridge, Southey, Wordsworth, — and finds the
promise of our future literature in the authors
of the "Pleasures of Memory" and the "Pleasures of Hope." Belonging himself essentially to
the Romantic movement, he would dissociate himself from the party; antagonism was better than
absorption. His high esteem for Pope was certainly genuine; it lasted during his entire life,
and arose partly from the fact that what was
lacking to himself as an artist and as a man he
found in Pope. He sprang upon his object; Pope
finessed with it. He was careless and splashy;
Pope strove to be exact and exquisite. He was
consumed with boundless ambition and desires;
Pope preached what he did not attain,— the wisdom of an equable temper, moderated wants and
wishes, submission to the rule of life, acceptance
of our place in the scale of being, good sense,
and, if possible, good sense with the added charm
of amiability.

In the first two cantos of "Childe Harold,"
which appeared in 1812, after his return from

Greece, Byron abandons Pope and the eighteenth century; he goes with the current of the time; he is essentially modern, though, half through humor and half through a notion of romance (for it was the season of romance), he wears a mediæval masquerade. We are not for a moment deluded by the fantastic garb; the "Childe" is a young Englishman of the opening years of the present century, who has the distinction of being a prey to consuming ardors and is touched by the melancholy which accompanies unsatisfied aspirations. In an addition which he made to his original preface Byron speaks with contempt of "the monstrous mummeries of the middle ages;" yet he affects an archaic costume. To find romance Scott had gone to the past; Byron undertook to show that the present is full of the elements of romance, — strangeness, picturesqueness, passion, adventures of love, adventures of war. The instant popularity of his poem proves how truly it was the offspring of the time. In it the junction between the Romantic and the Revolutionary movements, which gives much of its character to his work, was effected. His hero, as he tells us, was designed to be a kind of modern Timon; he had found satiety in excess of pleasure, and with this nineteenth-century Timon

melancholy takes the place of rage. But as the
mediævalism of the earlier cantos of "Childe
Harold" is only a transparent varnish, so the
misanthropy does not as yet go deep. It is indeed Byron's great capacity for enjoyment that
gives "Childe Harold" its real interest. He has
a feeling for the majesty of landscape, for men
and manners, for the life of society, for historical
associations, for contemporary events, for the
glory of literature and art, for the genius of nations and of individuals. The poem is a glorified
guide-book; but it is something more, for in the
person of his hero Byron creates a type which
represents modern romance, modern melancholy
(when the Revolutionary passions remained unsatisfied and the Revolutionary faiths were
obscured), and, with these, the capacities for
wide and varied pleasure proper to a time of
culture, of travel, of cosmopolitan sympathies
and interests.

It is sometimes forgotten, though it should
always be borne in mind, that the third and
fourth cantos of "Childe Harold" belong to a
later period than the first half of the poem. The
third canto was written in 1816, after Byron had
separated from his wife and had quitted his own
country. Instead of the half-fantastic melancholy

of the earlier cantos we have here the evidences
of real suffering.　The poet's passion is deeper;
his reflections are less obvious and superficial; his
power as a poet is no longer adolescent, but mature.　Byron's companionship with Shelley on
the Lake of Geneva helped to lift his spirit into
a higher and clearer atmosphere.　His capacity
for delight is not diminished, and indeed his
sense of pleasure seems enhanced by a closer
acquaintance with pain.　He snatches a joy more
eagerly.　The fourth canto, which tells of Italy,
carries the poem to a triumphant close.　The
hero is now frankly identified with the writer;
his misanthropy is Byron's own *Welt-schmerz;*
his rapture in nature, touched with a pantheistic
sentiment characteristic of the time, his joy in
man, and mingling with the joy his sense of the
pettiness of human life, are Byron's in their volume and their energy.　The chief value of the
poem lies not in this or that celebrated morsel of
description, which can be exhibited in a book of
extracts, but in the writer's deep interest in the
works and ways of humanity united with a revolt
against the world, and a scorn, not wholly feigned,
for human existence.　There are in it the ardor of
the Revolutionary epoch; and also the moral void
caused by a work of destruction which seemed

to have failed, and by the loss or the obscuration of the new faith in days of political reaction.

The Eastern Tales annexed a new province to Romantic poetry. Southey, indeed, in "Thalaba" and "Kehama" had found his themes in the Arabian wilds, and among the temples, the giant rivers, the inextricable forest-shades of India. But Southey's poems were written in an ethical spirit which was characteristically his own; they are tales of heroic duty and heroic fortitude, of vengeance that is just, and of the law of charity that supersedes the law of vengeance. Byron's are tales of passion. His heroes and heroines are those of Revolutionary romance; they are revolters against the social order, not like the humble martyrs of Southey's "Botany Bay Eclogues," but sublime in mysterious loves and hates, and dazzling in beauty or in pride, — Corsairs, Giaours, Pirates, a Lara, a Hugo, a Zuleika, a Gulnare. They are a law unto themselves; their noblest virtues are those found in connection with unrestrained abandonment to passion; they make an unqualified assertion of the rights of the individual will; their very love is a kind of egoism, or at best an egoism doubled in the person of another. Time, which cannot breathe the breath of change upon the highest works of art, has dealt hardly with these poems. Are we to think of them as no better than melodramas played by marionettes, turbaned and fierce of eye, or shaped after those ideals of feminine perfection which embellish some old Book of Beauty? The stage-properties are tarnished now; the vein of sentiment has run dry. But the Turk and the lady, the amorous pirate, the renegado, the rose of the harem, and the entire stock company were once as much alive as certain favorite heroes and heroines of contemporary fiction are at the present day. Perhaps Nora Helmer and Hedda Gabler may by and by repose in the old marionette box, and the wires by which their limbs are convulsed may have grown rusty; perhaps the sawdust already escapes from a clerical garb that was so fresh a few years since; perhaps a sprightly heroine of two or three seasons ago is no longer so atrociously sprightly. Let us feel towards Byron's Oriental figures with some tenderness, for they deserve it. It is worth while to set them on the stage again, and to hear them declaim their loves and hatreds, their rapture and revenge. How much of it all is real and how much is theatrical? and how has the manufacturer contrived to run together the false and the true, the pinchbeck and the gold? For all is not

unreal in these poems. Each was thrown off at
a heat, and the verse has often a fervid swiftness
of movement, like the stride of a racer; the
scenes are often strongly and vividly imagined;
true passion mingles with pseudo-passion; the
characters resemble one another, indeed, but they
exhibit a type which has an importance in the
history of European literature. Of the earlier
tales, perhaps the first in date presents the type
most powerfully. The darker and stronger
coloring of "The Giaour" certainly makes "The
Bride of Abydos" look pale and faint beside it.
In "The Prisoner of Chillon" fraternal affection takes the place of the passion of man and
woman; or if a heroine there be, she is named
Freedom, for whom the captive sighs with more
desire than mortal maiden could move in his afflicted heart. The other poem of captivity, "Ma-
zeppa," is a striking contrast; for here, instead of
pacing the narrow dungeon, heavy with stagnant
air, the captive is in swiftest motion, bound to
the rushing steed, while forest and stream and
wilderness and the solitary skies reel past him,
as he is borne afar from the haunts of men.
Shall we moralize it into an allegory of one bound
on the wild horse of passion and hurried into a
solitude of the soul?

Byron's residence in Italy produced some remarkable poems, other than dramatic, on Italian themes. And in these the temper of the Revolution may be easily discerned. The "Ode on Venice" laments the decay of the city of the sea under an alien tyranny, and hails the new world of America as the home of freedom, which has been banished from her ancient habitations by a coalition of kings, —

> "The name of Commonwealth is past and gone
>   O'er the three fractions of the groaning globe ;
> Venice is crush'd, and Holland deigns to own
>   A sceptre, and endures the purple robe ;
> If the free Switzer yet bestrides alone
> His chainless mountains, 't is but for a time,
> For tyranny of late is cunning grown,
> And in its own good season tramples down
> The sparkles of our ashes."

In "The Prophecy of Dante" the poet, writing in Dante's metre, tells of the glories and the shame of Italy ; but his copious rhetoric has little in common with the close-woven texture and austere beauty of the "Divine Comedy." Dante in the "Prophecy" is, like Byron, an exile ; and it was not of Dante only that the English singer thought when he foretold the day on which the poet's dust should be reclaimed by the Mother-country that had cast him forth. The foreign

tyranny of Italy is announced, and the one remaining hope for freedom is indicated in Italian
unity, —

> "What is there wanting, then, to set thee free,
>   And show thy beauty in its fullest light?
> To make the Alps impassable; and we,
>   Her sons, may do this with *one* deed, — Unite."

If Dante in Byron's poem is one who endures
the grief of exile, the Tasso of his impassioned
monologue is in yet more lamentable case, imprisoned as a madman in the hospital of Saint
Anna, severed from the princess whom in his
rashness he had loved, and — worst anguish —
aware that his genius is slowly decaying in the
penury of joy and hope. To these three poems
three cities of captive Italy lent their inspiration; they are the mourning chants of Venice,
Ravenna, Ferrara.

Byron's dramas are extraordinary *tours de
force* of a writer whose genius was not, in any high
degree, dramatic. Those which conform most
closely to the regular drama are the least excellent. His strong, imaginative feeling for history,
and his acquaintance with Venetian character
and Venetian local color, do not suffice to make
"Marino Faliero" or "The Two Foscari" an eminent historical play. To name them with Shake-

speare's tragedies is to reveal all their dramatic poverty; they cannot even compare with the masterpiece of Otway. The Eastern drama "Sardanapalus" interests the reader at least in its later acts, although the character of the monarch suddenly ennobled from a voluptuary to a hero, lacks depth and subtlety; there is spirit in the scenes of battle, and grandiosity in the close, when the defeated King of Nineveh and his Ionian slave and lover, Myrrha, mount the funeral pile in the vast abandoned palace. Those dramatic poems which make no pretence to be dramas in the strict sense of the word are more in harmony with Byron's genius. "Heaven and Earth," which tells of the loves of the angelic sons of God for the daughters of the race of Cain, is disfigured by its shapeless pseudo-lyrics; but a pervading sense of doom gives majesty to the poem, and the picture of the Deluge has been well compared to the treatment of the same subject in Poussin's impressive composition. "Cain" is a drama of intellectual and moral revolt; it tells the story of the first proud, insurgent spirit on earth, with his ardent love, his aspiring will, his passion for knowledge, his doubts and hopes and fears, his uprising against tyranny, his sudden crime, his condemnation, and his remorse. The poem is deficient in material action, but its dialogue is filled with what may be termed acts of the intellect; and in the flight of Lucifer and Cain through space, past starry worlds, to the realm of Hades, while daring doubts are ever proposed and are ever met by daring sophistries, a sense is conveyed to us of the grandeur and immensity of the universe, and at the same time a sense of the mysteries which encircle and baffle the human mind. "Heaven and Earth" and "Cain" we may call, as Byron would have it, not regular dramas, but "mysteries." "Manfred" is a "dramatic poem." Once again the protagonist is a revolter against the laws of life. The shadow of an inexpiable crime and a mortal sorrow broods over him. He has sought for light and help in forbidden knowledge; he has subjected to his spells the elemental spirits; but he has found that those who know the most have the deepest cause to mourn over the fatal truth that the Tree of Knowledge is not the Tree of Life. Humanity is here shown in antagonism with the conditions of its existence. The greatness of man is at strife with the inadequacy of the means to support that greatness. This discordant, unintelligible being — man — is surrounded

with immortal beauty and grandeur, which make
him only the more sensible of the discordance
between his aspirations and his attainments.
The glories of Alpine landscape, with sunrise
and sunset among the mountains, the eagle on
the wing, the avalanche, the glacier, the rainbow-
enchanted torrent, form a splendid environment
for the melancholy figure of the feudal lord and
Magian, to whom love has brought only remorse,
and in whose spirit knowledge has engendered
only sorrow.

It is in ways which are indirect that the spirit
of the Revolution, united with the genius of
Romance, appears to most advantage in the
poetry of Byron. "The Age of Bronze," written
at Genoa in 1823, deals immediately with politics, and the poem is not one of his happier
achievements. Napoleon, now the caged eagle
squabbling for his rations, was once upon the
wing, a power of freedom in the world. "He
burst," says Byron, "the chains of millions, and
for what? To renew the fetters which he had
broken. And yet the spark of liberty is not ex-
tinct. In the South American republics, in Spain,
in Greece, it lives and works. Byron exults in
the thought of the uprising of the peoples; he
derides the policy of the Holy Alliance. Turning

to England, he sees the landed interest wholly
devoted to the raising of rents; the Church
weeping like Niobe over her offspring, — tithes;
the stock-jobbers on 'Change, the Jew speculators,
making their market out of the hopes and fears
of nations; and for each the poet has some line
or some phrase of indignant rhetoric. He concludes with an outburst of laughter at the ultra-
loyalty of the Highland kilts of the city-knight,
Sir William Curtis, — "Vich Ian Alderman," —
worn at Holyrood in the presence of King George
IV. The satire which strives to be vigorous has
an air of exhaustion. Some of the bronze of the
age described by Byron entered into his poem.

From Hookham Frere, and through his own
versification of Pulci's "Morgante Maggiore,"
Byron had learnt the use of the *ottava rima.*
Its springing gait suited well with the gay superciliousness, the light insolence of "The Vision
of Judgment." To explode with inextinguish-
able laughter such an arch-respectability as the
Poet Laureate had in it something inexpressibly
exhilarating.   Never had Byron written with
greater animation; the serious purpose under-
lying a superficial profanity suited his genius.
Beneath the burlesque handling of things sacred
appears the better spirit of the poet in the zeal

with which he pleads for what to him was in truth sacred, — the cause of political freedom. But it is in "Don Juan" that the whole of Byron is deployed, — the evil and the good, the spirit that sinks and the spirit that soars. Whoever named it the "Odyssey of Immorality" suggests only half the truth. It is undoubtedly a poem of moral rebellion, and well expresses the temper of a time when old reverences were discredited, and ancient landmarks had been removed; yet a certain fire of the ideal lives throughout the poem. Licentious, cynical, irreverent, shameless, — the accustomed counts of accusation may all be admitted; yet it is also inspired by not ignoble passion. Its morality, if one desires to seek for this, may be found in a scorn for base things of the world which obstruct generous effort and sap generous faith, and with which Byron waxes indignant, partly because he has himself suffered from their rule or influence. He cannot for more than an hour, or perhaps a moment, believe in love, constancy, patriotism, virtue; yet he knows that these are the life of life, and he turns with bitter mockery to revenge himself on the society of worldlings and of hypocrites which has helped to make him a mocker and a sceptic. It is a mistake to suppose that what is best in "Don Juan" can be severed from what is worst, and be presented apart. What is best lives in what is worst. Byron's cynicism is his testimony to the truth that man must live by faith; his bitterness of spirit means that to move sanely and joyously in a moral void is impossible. At the last moment his nobler self revolted against the baseness not only around him but within him, and it was the champion of Greek liberty who fell asleep at Missolonghi. In his delirium he was mounting a breach,—"Forwards, forwards, courage, follow my example." When calm returned, he was heard to murmur: "Poor Greece! . . . I have given her my time, my means, my health — and now I give her my life! What could I do more?" As the day drew towards sunset, he spoke: "Now I shall go to sleep;" after which no word was uttered.

> "This should have been a noble creature : he
>   Hath all the energy which would have made
>   A goodly frame of glorious elements,
>   Had they been wisely mingled ; as it is
>   It is an awful chaos — light and darkness,
>   And mind and dust, and passions and pure thoughts
>   Mix'd, and contending without end or order."

These lines from "Manfred" might serve for Byron's epitaph.

Having told the story of Shelley's life in great detail, and having summed up my general impression of the man and his work in a brief study,[1] I shall not attempt to add anything to what I have already written. The view which presents Shelley as a leader of thought and that which sees in him a mere visionary are assuredly alike erroneous. To nineteenth-century thought he did not contribute a single original idea of importance. A definite body of doctrine lies behind the colors and melodies of his verse, but this is derived from Godwin and the French philosophers who prepared the way of Revolution. In essentials nothing is changed. Their errors and their illusions were Shelley's. But it must be added that the truths of which their writings became the vehicles were also his. And as these truths were important and have been powerfully operative during a hundred years, a poet who apprehended them and vitalized them by his passions and his imagination cannot be rightly considered a dreamer or a phantast. Some, indeed, of Shelley's hopes for society were illusive. The conception of the ideal man of a future golden age as

[1] Transcripts and Studies, pp. 75–111: "Last Words on Shelley."

> " Equal, unclassed, tribeless, and nationless,
>   Exempt from awe, worship, degree,"

is a false conception. But some of his visions
were prophetic, and society is now visibly nearer
to their fulfilment than when he gave them
utterance. He did not anticipate a speedy at-
tainment of what the future holds in store. His
expectations were moderate. " The great thing,"
he wrote, " is to hold the balance between popular impatience and tyrannical obstinacy. . . . I
am one of those whom nothing will satisfy, but
who are ready to be partially satisfied in all that
is practicable." He held that the progress of
society cannot but be slow and gradual; and at
the same time he believed that it is well to have
before us ideals of what is very far off, both as
guiding lights, and as encouragements to effort
and to fortitude.

Progress, fraternity, equality, freedom, — these
high-sounding words have been as wind to in-
flate much soaring rhetoric; but they are great
words, with most substantial meanings, if we
consider them aright. Some of their true significance was interpreted by the poetry of Shelley.
" In the earlier years of our century " — I must
be my own plagiarist — " the democratic movement concerned itself too exclusively with the

individual and his rights, and regarded too little
his duties, affections, and privileges as a member
of society. It is greatly to the advantage of
Shelley's work as a poet, and greatly to his
credit as a man, that he assigns to love — that
which links us to our fellows — some of the
power and authority which Godwin ascribes to
reason alone. The French Revolution had been
in a great measure a destruction of the ancient
order of society, and such poetry as Byron's,
sympathizing with the Revolution, is too reckless
an assertion of individual freedom. Shelley was
deeply infected with the same errors. But it is
part of the glory of his poetry that in some
degree he anticipated the sentiment of the second
half of our century, when we desire more to construct or reconstruct than to destroy. Shelley's
ideas of a reconstruction of society are indeed
at times vague or visionary ; but there is always
present in his poetry the sentiment or feeling
which tends to reconstruction, the feeling of
genuine love for men and concern for their
higher interests. With him the word "fraternity" is at least as potent as the word "liberty."
In Byron we find an expression of the Revolution on its negative side, — not wholly, but in
the main ; in Shelley we find this, but in the

main an expression of the Revolution on its positive side. As the wave of revolution rolls onward, driven forth from the vast volcanic upheaval in France, and as it becomes a portion of the literary movement of Great Britain, its dark and hissing crest may be the poetry of Byron ; but over the tumultuous wave hangs an iris of beauty and promise, and that foam-bow of hope, flashing and failing, and ever reappearing as the wave sweeps on, is the poetry of Shelley." [1]

So I wrote several years since. It was a temperate estimate of the value of Shelley's work. If it fail to satisfy admirers who will accept no reserves, and if it seem extravagant to those who have no perception of the stronger and saner side of his character and genius, perhaps it is not the less likely on this account to be an approximation to the truth.

[1] Transcripts and Studies, pp. 96, 97.